SLOW COOKER
COOKBOOK

for beginners

**1500 +
DAYS OF EFFORTLESS HOME-COOKED
MEALS MADE ON SLOW COOKING**

**FROM BEGINNER TO MASTER WITH
DELICIOUS RECIPES**

DANNY MOORE

CONTENTS

INTRODUCTION

Without a doubt, the slow cooker is an incredible kitchen appliance that will become essential in your daily meal planning. The slow cooker will allow you to prepare delicious meals for yourself, family and friends effortlessly and without spending hours in the kitchen. You will save time, which you can devote to other activities, but at the same time you are guaranteed to eat healthy meals thanks to slow cooking. This appliance will also help you a lot when you have to follow a specific diet, planning an effective eating plan, and will become the kitchen assistant you have always wanted. The use of a low temperature also ensures that the correct cooking point is reached. For the modern cook, low-temperature cooking offers numerous advantages and will definitely *change your cooking life*.

WHY CHOOSING SLOW COOKING?

ENHANCE FLAVOR Cooking ingredients for several hours with spices, herbs and other seasonings creates vegetables and proteins that burst with delicious flavors. This slow process allows flavors to mature and deepen for a better eating experience.

TIME SAVING Cooking at home takes a great deal of time: prepping, sautéing, stirring, raising and lowering the heat, and watching the meal so that it is not over or undercooked. If you don't have time on your hands, you may find yourself choosing convenience foods

instead of healthy choices. Slow cookers allow you to do other activities while the meal is cooking. You can put

your ingredients in the slow cooker in the morning and come home with a perfectly cooked meal.

CONVENIENCE In addition to the time-saving aspect, using a slow stove can free up your stove and oven for other dishes. This can be very helpful with large holiday meals or when you want to serve a meal with multiple dishes.

REDUCE HEAT PRODUCTION Slow stoves use about a third of the energy of conventional cooking methods, only a little more energy than a traditional light bulb.

SUPPORT HEALTHY EATING Cooking your food at high heat can reduce the nutritional profile (per serving) of your food, breaking down and removing most vitamins, minerals and antioxidants while producing unhealthy chemical compounds that can contribute to disease.

MONEY SAVING Slow stoves save you money because of the low amount of electricity they use and because the best ingredients for slow cooking are the least expensive cuts of beef and the sturdiest, most inexpensive vegetables. The toughest cuts of meat - brisket, beef, shank - break down beautifully and become fork tender. Another cost-saving benefit is that most 6-quart slow stoves will produce enough of a recipe to stretch meals for at least two days. Leftovers are one of the best ways to save money.

TIPS AND TRICKS FOR SLOW COOKING

The slow cooker is simple to use, but you can get amazing results with a few tips and techniques. First, always read the user manual included in the slow-cooker box, so take the time to read everything completely before using a new device.

Grease the slow cooker insert **before cooking**. Cleaning the insert of a slow cooker can be a challenge, so grease the insert, even for soups and stews. Or alternatively use slow cooker liner to clean it up much easier

Do not scrub the insert **with abrasive brushes** or scrape off pieces of cooked food because you will ruin its nonstick surface

Add dairy products and herbs at the end of the cooking process. Actually, fresh dairy products and herbs do not hold up well during long cooking times. Dairy products crack and create a grainy, unpleasant texture, and herbs lose their flavor, color and texture. So remember to add them only at the end

Always **cut ingredients into similar sized pieces**. Slow cookers are not meant to be used for staggered cooking recipes, such as stir-fries, where more delicate ingredients are added last to avoid overcooking. Similar sized pieces mean your ingredients will be ready at the same time and your meals will be cooked evenly.

No need to use **expensive cuts of meat**; since this cooking method allows to get tender and juicy meats you can grab low cost cuts and let it cook all day to get full-of-flavor meals

Never use frozen meats or poultry. Ingredients in slow cookers must reach 140°F within 4 hours for food safety, so large cuts of meat or poultry must be completely thawed. You can add small frozen items such as meatballs to a slow cooker because these can come to temperature in this time frame.

Resume cooking after a power outage of more than two hours. Power outages can occur in any season and, for food safety reasons, you should err on the side of caution. If an outage lasts more than two hours, especially during the first few hours of cooking, you must discard the food because the time spent in the food danger zone (40°F to 140°F) will have been too long. If the interruption is less than two hours and occurs after the food has been cooking for at least four hours, then you can resume cooking until the end of the original time or transfer the food to a pot or casserole and finish it on the stove or in the oven. When in doubt, throw the food away.

Use the recommended high altitude cooking times. As with most other cooking methods, slow cookers need more cooking time if you live above 3,000 feet in elevation. The liquid in the slow cooker will simmer at a lower temperature, so high temperature settings are recommended, or if you can program the slow cooker, set it to hold the food at 200°F or higher. You can also use a temperature probe set to 165°F internal temperature if your slow cooker has this feature.

CHAPTER 1. BREAKFAST

Tomatoes Asparagus Frittata

Prep Time: 15 minutes | Cooking Time: 6 hours

Ingredients (6 Servings):

- 12 large eggs
- 2 tbsp unsalted butter, ghee, or olive oil
- ¼ cup heavy cream
- 1½ cups shredded sharp white Cheddar cheese, divided
- ½ cup grated Parmesan cheese
- 16 cherry tomatoes
- 16 asparagus spears

Directions:

Glaze the inside of the slow cooker with the butter.

In the slow cooker, beat the eggs, then whisk in the heavy cream, salt, and pepper.

Add ¾ cup of Cheddar cheese and the Parmesan cheese and stir to mix.

Sprinkle the remaining ¾ cup of Cheddar cheese over the top. Scatter the cherry tomatoes over the frittata. Arrange the asparagus spears decoratively over the top. Cook within 6 hours on low or 3 hours on soaring. Serve.

Nutrition (per Serving): Calories 350 Fat 29g Carbs 4g Protein 24g

Low Carb Zucchini Bread

Prep Time: 15 minutes | Cooking Time: 3 H 10 minutes

Ingredients (12 Servings):

- 3 eggs
- ½ cup walnuts, chopped
- 2 cups zucchini, shredded
- 2 tsp vanilla
- ½ cup pure all-purpose sweetener
- 1/3 cup coconut oil, softened
- 1 ½ tsp baking powder
- 2 tsp cinnamon
- 1/3 cup coconut flour
- 1 cup almond flour

Directions:

Mix the almond flour, baking powder, cinnamon, and coconut flour in a bowl. Set aside.

Whisk eggs, vanilla, sweetener, and oil in another bowl. Put the dry batter into the wet and fold well. Add walnut and zucchini and fold well.

Pour the batter into the silicone bread pan. Place the bread pan into the slow cooker on the rack. Cook on high within 3 hours. Cut the bread loaf into the slices and serve.

Nutrition (per Serving): Calories 174 Fat 15.4 g Carbs 5.8 g Protein 5.3 g

Creamy Breakfast Casserole

Prep Time: 15 minutes | Cooking Time: 6 hours

Ingredients (8 Servings):

- 8 large eggs, beaten
- 1 tbsp unsalted butter
- 1 cup heavy (whipping) cream
- 1½ cups shredded sharp Cheddar cheese, divided
- ½ cup grated Romano cheese
- 8 oz thick-cut ham, diced
- ¾ head broccoli, cut into small florets
- ½ onion, diced

Directions:

Grease the slow cooker with the butter. Whisk the eggs, heavy cream, ½ cup of Cheddar cheese, the Romano cheese inside the slow cooker. Stir in the ham, broccoli, and onion. Put the remaining 1 cup of Cheddar cheese over the top. Cook within 6 hours on low or 3 hours on high. Serve hot.

Nutrition (per Serving): Calories 425 Fat 31g Carbs 7g Protein 28g

Hash Brown Breakfast Casserole

Prep Time: 15 minutes | Cooking Time: 6 hours

Ingredients (6 Servings):

- 10 large eggs
- 1 tbsp unsalted butter
- ½ cup heavy cream
- ½ tsp ground mustard
- 1 head cauliflower, shredded or minced
- 2 onions, diced

- 10 oz cooked sausage links, sliced
- 2 ½ cups shredded Cheddar cheese, divided

Directions:

Grease the slow cooker with the butter.

Beat the eggs, then whisk in heavy cream, and the ground mustard in a large bowl. Spread about one-third of the cauliflower in an even layer in the bottom of the cooker. Layer one-third of the onions over the cauliflower, then one-third of the sausage, and top with ½ cup of Cheddar cheese. Season with salt and pepper. Repeat twice. Pour the egg batter evenly over the layered ingredients, then sprinkle the remaining ½ cup Cheddar cheese on top—Cook within 6 hours on low. Serve hot.

Nutrition (per Serving): Calories 523 Fat 40g Carbs 7g Protein 33g

Onion Broccoli Quiche

Prep Time: 15 minutes | Cooking Time: 2 H 25 minutes

Ingredients (8 Servings):

- 8 eggs
- 2 cups cheese, shredded and divided
- 8 oz cream cheese
- 1/4 tsp onion powder
- 2 cups broccoli, cut into florets

Directions:

Add broccoli into the boiling water and cook for 3 minutes. Drain well and set aside to cool.

Add eggs, cream cheese, and onion powder in mixing bowl and beat until well combined.

Spray slow cooker from inside using cooking spray. Add cooked broccoli into the slow cooker then sprinkle half cup cheese. Pour egg mixture over broccoli and cheese mixture.

Cook on high within 2 hours and 15 minutes. Once it is done, then sprinkle the remaining cheese and cover for 10 minutes or until cheese melted. Serve.

Nutrition (per Serving): Calories 296 Fat 24.3 g Carb 3.9 g Protein 16.4 g

Thyme Sausage Squash

Prep Time: 15 minutes | Cooking Time: 6 hours

Ingredients (4 Servings):

- 14 oz smoked chicken sausage, thinly sliced
- ¼ cup vegetable broth
- 1 onion, halved and sliced
- ½ medium butternut squash, peeled, diced
- 1 small green bell pepper, diced
- ½ small red bell pepper, diced
- ½ small yellow bell pepper, diced
- 2 tsp fresh thyme or ½ tsp dried thyme, crushed
- 2 tbsp olive oil
- 1 cup shredded Swiss cheese

Directions:

Combine the olive oil, sausage, broth, onion, butternut squash, bell peppers, thyme in the slow cooker. Toss to mix. Cook within 6 hours on low. Before serving, sprinkle the Swiss cheese over the top, cover, and cook for about 3 minutes more to melt the cheese.

Nutrition (per Serving): Calories 402 Fat 28g Carbs 12g Protein 27g

Sausage & Peppers

Prep Time: 15 minutes | Cooking Time: 6 hours

Ingredients (4 Servings):

- 4 green bell peppers, cleaned and sliced
- 6 garlic cloves, minced
- 2 large yellow onions
- 28 oz canned unsalted crushed tomatoes
- ¼ cup of water
- 1 bay leaf
- 2 lb. uncooked Sausage Links, mild or spicy
- ¼ tsp dried oregano
- ½ tsp crushed red pepper flakes

Directions:

Peel the onions and halve, then cut. Add the garlic and sliced onion into the slow cooker.

Remember to spray the slow cooker with oil. Add the sliced bell peppers, crushed red pepper flakes, dried oregano, 1 can crushed tomatoes, and water to the slow cooker Stir to coat and distribute the liquid evenly. Take out almost half of the peppers and the onion mixture into a bowl. Dip the uncooked sausage in the middle and then add the peppers and the onions back to the slow cooker. Put the bay leaf, then cover, set on low, and cook for 6 hours. Serve hot.

Nutrition (per Serving): Calories 456 Fat 36g Carbs 15g Fiber 4g Protein 24g

Breakfast (Sausage) Casserole

Prep Time: 15 minutes | Cooking Time: 3 hours

Ingredients (6 Servings):

- 1 lb. pork sausage
- ½ cup chopped green bell pepper
- ½ cup chopped red bell pepper
- 10 large eggs
- ½ cup coconut milk
- 1 tbsp yeast

- 1 tsp dry rubbed sage
- 1 tsp dried thyme
- ½ tsp garlic powder
- ½ cup sliced red onion

Directions:

Heat-up a medium cast-iron skillet over medium heat for 2 minutes. Add the pork sausage, then break it into small crumbles. Cook for 3 minutes. Stir in the thyme, sage, and garlic powder. Cook for an additional 5 minutes. Turn the heat off.

Stir in the bell peppers and the chopped onion. Add the pork and vegetable mixture into the bottom of the slow cooker.

Whisk the coconut milk, yeast, and the eggs until the eggs are well incorporated together in a large bowl. Pour it into the slow cooker on top of the pork mixture. Cook on low for 2 to 3 hours. Chop into 6 servings.

Nutrition (per Serving): Calories 377 Carbs 4g Fat 25g Protein 23g

Stuffed Breakfast Peppers

Prep Time: 15 minutes | Cooking Time: 2 hours

Ingredients (3 Servings):

- 3 bell peppers halved and seeded
- 3 eggs
- ½ cup milk
- 2 tbsp chopped green onion
- ¼ cup chopped frozen spinach thawed, squeezed dry
- ¾ cup shredded cheddar cheese
- ½ cup finely chopped ham

Directions:

Line slow cooker with tin foil. Arrange the peppers in the slow cooker and fill with the remaining fixings. Cook on low within 2 hours. Serve.

Nutrition (per Serving): Calories 360 Carbs 13g Protein 28g Fat 25g

Cheese & Sausage Breakfast

Prep Time: 15 minutes | Cooking Time: 2 hours

Ingredients (6 Servings):

- 10 eggs
- 2 tbsp butter, softened
- 8 oz breakfast sausage
- 1 lb. sweet potatoes, peeled and cubed
- 1 cup milk
- 4 oz shredded cheddar cheese

Directions:

Coat the slow cooker using softened butter.

Sauté in a large skillet over medium heat, the breakfast sausage until cooked through and browned, about 10 minutes. Put the sweet potatoes into a microwave-safe bowl. Add 1 tbsp water and cover bowl with a damp paper towel—microwave on high within 3 to 4 minutes.

Arrange the sausage and sweet potatoes in the bottom of the slow cooker.

Toss eggs, black pepper, milk, and salt to combine. Add the cheese; stir to mix very well.

Pour the egg and cheese mixture over sausage and sweet potatoes. Then put 2 layers of paper towels below the slow cooker lid before. Cook on high for 2 hours. Slice and serve.

Nutrition (per Serving): Calories 326 Carbs 18g Protein 21g Fat 16g

Mushrooms, Beef, & Zucchini Toast

Prep Time: 15 minutes | Cooking Time: 8 hours

Ingredients (8 Servings):

- 3 lb. boneless beef chuck roast
- 2 cups vegetable broth
- 5-7 radishes, cut into halves
- 1½ cups cauliflower florets
- ½ cup chopped celery
- 1/3 cup zucchini rounds
- ¼ cup chopped yellow bell pepper
- 1 tsp xanthan gum (optional to thicken the gravy)
- 1 tsp garlic powder
- 1 tbsp avocado oil
- 1 small onion chopped
- ½ cup sliced mushrooms
- 2 tbsp tomato paste

Directions:

Season the garlic powder, and salt. Let it stand alone for about 25 to 30 minutes. Add oil to a large skillet on medium-high heat. Add the roast; sear until brown, about 4 minutes on all sides. Add the diced mushrooms and onions; let them cook for about 1 to 2 minutes until sweet-smelling. Transfer the roast and the onions to the bottom of a slow cooker, then pour in the broth; then cook on high for 4 hours or low for 7 hours. Add the vegetables: zucchini, celery, turnips, bell peppers, and cauliflower. Set it again for about 1 hour. Serve hot with gravy.

Nutrition (per Serving): Calories 345 Fat 21g Carbs 4g Protein 34g

Slow cooker Keto Muffins

Prep Time: 15 minutes | Cooking Time: 2 hours

Ingredients (4 Servings):

- 3 tbsp almond flour
- 1/2 tbsp coconut flour
- 1 tbsp butter
- 1 egg

- 1/2 tsp baking soda

Directions:

Take a medium-sized skillet, melt the butter. It usually takes 20-30 seconds. Pour coconut, almond flour, and egg into the melted butter and stir everything well. Remove skillet from the heat and add baking soda. Coat the slow cooker with cooking spray. Pour the mixture. Put on low for 2 hours. Check the readiness with a fork. Remove the baked muffin from the slow cooker and eat with bacon slices, cheese, or other breakfast staples.

Nutrition (per Serving): Calories 28 Carbs 3g Fat 5g Protein 7g

Cauliflower Casserole with Goat Cheese

Prep Time: 15 minutes | Cooking Time: 3 hours

Ingredients (8 Servings):

- 6 cups cauliflower florets
- 2 oz goat cheese crumbled
- 3 tsp olive oil
- 1 tsp dried oregano

For the Sauce:

- 2 bay leaves
- 1 tsp olive oil
- 2 garlic cloves
- 1 (28 oz) can crushed tomatoes

Directions:

Grease the slow cooker with cooking spray, put the cauliflower on its bottom, add olive oil, oregano, and pepper. Cook on the low setting within 2 hours until the cauliflower florets get tender and a little bit brown color. For making the sauce: Take a medium-sized skillet, heat the olive oil, add garlic and cook 1 minute, stir it thoroughly all the time. Add the crushed tomatoes and bay leaves; let it simmer for some minutes. Remove the bay leaves, dress with pepper and salt. Put the sauce over the cauliflower florets in the slow cooker once the time is over. Spread the Goat cheese over the dish, cover the slow cooker, and continue cooking for 1 hour on low. Serve warm!

Nutrition (per Serving): Calories 170 Carbs 10g Fat 13g Protein 7g

Greek Eggs Breakfast Casserole

Prep Time: 15 minutes | Cooking Time: 5 hours

Ingredients (6 Servings):

- 10 whisked eggs
- ½ cup whole milk
- 1 tbsp red onion
- 1 tsp garlic powder
- ½ cup Sun-dried tomatoes
- 2 cups spinach
- ½ cup Feta Cheese crushed

Directions:

Whisk the eggs in a bowl. Add milk and stir to combine. Add the minced onion and garlic.

Add dried tomatoes and spinach. Pour all the batter into the slow cooker, add Feta cheese.

Set to cook on the low setting within 5-6 hours. Serve.

Nutrition (per Serving): Calories 223 Carbs 5g Fat 17g Protein 18g

Turkish Breakfast Eggs

Prep Time: 15 minutes | Cooking Time: 4 hours

Ingredients (4 Servings):

- 4 eggs
- 1 slice bread
- 10 cherry tomatoes
- 2 onions, chopped
- 2 red bell peppers, sliced
- 4 tbsp natural yogurt
- 1 tsp red chili flakes
- 1 tbsp olive oil
- 2 tbsp milk
- A bunch of parsley, chopped

Directions:

Grease the slow cooker using oil. Heat-up, the oil, add the onions, pepper, and chili in a large skillet, then stir. Cook until the veggies begin to soften. Transfer it in the Slow cooker, then add the cherry tomatoes and bread, stir everything well. Cook on low for 4 hours—season with fresh parsley and yogurt.

Nutrition (per Serving): Calories 123 Carbs 12g Fat 5g Protein 6g

Mexican Breakfast Casserole

Prep Time: 15 minutes | Cooking Time: 5 hours

Ingredients (5 Servings):

- 5 eggs
- 6 oz pork sausage, cooked, drained
- ½ cup milk
- ½ tsp garlic powder
- 2 jalapeños, finely chopped
- ½ tsp ground cumin
- ½ tsp ground coriander
- 1 ½ cups chunky salsa
- 1 ½ cup pepper Jack cheese, shredded
- ¼ cup fresh cilantro

Directions:

Coat the slow cooker with cooking spray. Mix the eggs plus milk in a bowl. Add garlic powder, cumin, coriander, and sausage and mix well.

Pour the mixture into the slow cooker. Set the slow cooker on Low within 4-5 hours or on High for 2-3 hours. Place toppings of your choice and serve.

Nutrition (per Serving): Calories 320 Fat 24.1 g Carbs 5.2 g Protein 17.9 g

Almond Berry Muffins

Prep Time: 15 minutes | Cooking Time: 3 hours

Ingredients (3 Servings):

- 1 cup almond flour
- 1 large egg
- 3 drops stevia
- ¼ cup fresh blueberries
- ¼ tsp lemon zest, grated
- 1 tsp lemon juice
- ½ cup heavy whipping cream
- 2 tbsp butter, melted
- ½ tsp baking powder

Directions:

Whisk the egg into a bowl. Add the rest of the fixing, and mix.

Pour batter into lined or greased muffin molds. Pour up to ¾ of the cup.

Pour 6 oz of water into the slow cooker. Place an aluminum foil at the bottom, and the muffin molds inside. Set the slow cooker on High within 2-3 hours. Let it cool in the cooker for a while. Remove from the cooker. Loosen the edges of the muffins. Serve.

Nutrition (per Serving): Calories 373 Fat 35g Carbs 9g Protein 10 g

Veggie Mix Omelet

Prep Time: 15 minutes | Cooking Time: 1 H 40 minutes

Ingredients (4 Servings):

- 6 eggs
- 1 tsp parsley, dried
- 1 tsp garlic powder
- 1 bell pepper, diced
- ½ cup onion, sliced
- 1 cup spinach
- ½ cup almond milk, unsweetened
- 4 egg whites

Directions:

Grease the slow cooker from inside using cooking spray. Whisk egg whites, eggs, parsley, garlic powder, almond milk, in a large bowl. Stir in bell peppers, spinach, and onion. Pour egg batter into the slow cooker. Cook on high within 90 minutes or until egg sets. Cut into the slices and serve.

Nutrition (per Serving): Calories 200 Fat 13.9 g Carbs 5.8 g Protein 13.4 g

Pesto Scrambled Eggs

Prep Time: 5 minutes | Cooking Time: 4 hours

Ingredients (3 Servings):

- 3 eggs, beaten
- 1 tbsp butter
- 1 tbsp organic green pesto sauce
- 2 tbsp sour cream, full-fat

Directions:

In a mixing bowl, combine all fixings. Cook in the slow cooker on high within 2 hours or on low for 4 hours. Halfway before the cooking time, use a fork to break the eggs into small pieces. Continue cooking until eggs are well done. Serve.

Nutrition (per Serving): Calories 147 Carbs 3.3g Protein 10.4g Fat 11.5g

Kale & Cheese Omelet

Prep Time: 5 minutes | Cooking Time: 3 hours

Ingredients (2 Servings):

- 4 eggs, beaten
- 2 tbsp onion, chopped
- 2 tsp olive oil
- 3 oz kale, chopped
- 1/3 cup white cheese, grated

Directions:

Mix all fixings in a bowl. Put it in the slow cooker. Cook on high within 2 hours or on low for 3 hours.

Nutrition (per Serving): Calories 254 Carbs 2.1g Protein 14.5g Fat 26.2g

Egg Casserole with Cheese, and Herbs

Prep Time: 5 minutes | Cooking Time: 3 hours

Ingredients (4 Servings):

- 8 eggs
- 2 tbsp milk
- 3 tbsp sun-dried tomatoes, chopped
- 2 tbsp onion, minced
- 2 tbsp basil, chopped
- 1 tbsp thyme leaves
- 1 cup mixed grated cheeses

Directions:

Mix all ingredients in a bowl. Put it inside your slow cooker and set to cook on high for 2 hours or low for 3 hours.

Nutrition (per Serving): Calories 140 Carbs 4.7g Protein 10.9g Fat 8.89g

Kale, Mushrooms, & Caramelized Onions

Prep Time: 10 minutes | Cooking Time: 4 hours

Ingredients (6 Servings):

- 8 large eggs, beaten
- 2 tsp olive oil
- ½ tbsp onion, caramelized

- 1 red bell pepper, diced
- 1 cup mushrooms, sliced
- 2 cups kale, chopped
- ¼ cup milk
- 2 cups cheese, shredded

Directions:

Place all fixings in the slow cooker. Cook on high within 3 hours or on low for 4 hours.

Nutrition (per Serving): Calories 255 Carbs 4.6g Protein 16.1g Fat 21.3g

Egg and Cheese Casserole with Squash

Prep Time: 5 minutes | Cooking Time: 4 hours

Ingredients (4 Servings):

- 8 large eggs, beaten
- 2 tbsp milk
- 1 tsp olive oil
- 1 red onion, diced
- 2 medium chayote squash, grated
- ½ small red bell pepper, diced
- ¼ cup low-fat cottage cheese
- 2 cups grated cheesed

Directions:

Combine all fixings in a mixing bowl. Pour into the slow cooker. Cook on high within 3 hours or on low for 4 hours.

Nutrition (per Serving): Calories 389 Carbs 6.3g Protein 35.2g Fat 33.6g

Sausage and Kale

Prep Time: 5 minutes | Cooking Time: 4 hours

Ingredients (10 Servings):

- 10 eggs, beaten
- 2 ½ cups milk
- 2 tbsp fresh oregano, minced

- 2 lb. breakfast sausages, sliced
- 1 bunch kale, into pieces
- 16 oz white mushrooms, sliced
- 2 cups Monterey Jack cheese, grated

Directions:

Mix all fixings in a large mixing bowl until well combined. Pour into the slow cooker and close the lid. Set to cook on high within 3 hours or low for 4 hours.

Nutrition (per Serving): Calories 451 Carbs 4.5g Protein 32.3g Fat 37.4g

Egg Cake Recipe with Veggies

Prep Time: 10 minutes | Cooking Time: 4 hours

Ingredients (6 Servings):

- 10 eggs, beaten
- ¼ cup milk
- ¼ cup almond flour
- 1 garlic clove, minced
- 1 cup kale, chopped
- 1 red bell pepper, chopped
- ¾ cup mozzarella cheese, grated
- 1 green onion, chopped

Directions:

In a mixing bowl, combine all fixings. Pour into the slow cooker. Cook on high within 4 hours or on low for 6 hours. Serve.

Nutrition (per Serving): Calories 206 Carbs 3.1g Protein 14.3g Fat 15.6g

Feta Cheese & Kale Breakfast Casserole

Prep Time: 5 minutes | Cooking Time: 4 hours

Ingredients (6 Servings):

- 10 oz kale, chopped
- 2 tsp olive oil
- ¾ cup feta cheese, crumbled

- 10 eggs, beaten

Directions:

Mix all fixings in a large mixing bowl until well combined. Put the batter inside the slow cooker, then cook on high for 3 hours or low for 4 hours.

Nutrition (per Serving): Calories 197 Carbs 4g Protein 12.2g Fat 13.4g

Cauliflower & Ham Casserole

Prep Time: 5 minutes | Cooking Time: 4 hours

Ingredients (6 Servings):

- 12 eggs, beaten
- 1 head cauliflower, grated
- 1 cup ham, cubed
- ½ cup mozzarella cheese, grated
- ½ cup cheddar cheese, grated
- 2 onions, chopped

Directions:

Mix all fixings in a bowl. Pour into the slow cooker. Cook on high within 3 hours or on low for 4 hours.

Nutrition (per Serving): Calories 242 Carbs 5.2g Protein 28.1g Fat 16.4g

Sausage-Stuffed Eggplants

Prep Time: 10 minutes | Cooking Time: 6 hours

Ingredients (6 Servings):

- 12 oz sausage links, chopped
- 3 medium eggplants, sliced
- 2 garlic cloves, minced
- 2 tbsp rosemary, fresh
- 6 slices mozzarella cheese

Directions:

Mix all items in a bowl. Line a foil at the bottom of the slow cooker. Grease with cooking spray. Pour into the slow cooker and cook on low for 6 hours or on high for 4 hours. Serve.

Nutrition (per Serving): Calories 271 Carbs 6.3g Protein 16.83g Fat 25.9g

Zucchini Sausage Breakfast "Bake"

Prep Time: 5 minutes | Cooking Time: 4 hours

Ingredients (8 Servings):

- 8 oz cream cheese
- 8 large eggs
- 1 lb. Italian sausages, chopped
- ½ cup coconut flour
- 2 tsp baking powder
- 2 small zucchinis, grated
- 4 garlic cloves, minced
- 1 cup cheese, shredded

Directions:

Mix all fixings in a bowl. Set in the slow cooker; cook within 3 hours on high or on low for 4 hours.

Nutrition (per Serving): Calories 344 Carbs 6.3g Protein 21g Fat 27g

Cheddar Jalapeno Breakfast Sausages

Prep Time: 5 minutes | Cooking Time: 6 hours

Ingredients (12 Servings):

- 12 medium-sized breakfast sausages
- 1 jalapeno pepper, chopped
- ½ cup cheddar cheese, grated
- ¼ cup heavy cream

Directions:

Mix all items in a bowl, then put it into the slow cooker. Set to cook on low for 6 hours or on high for 4 hours. Garnish with parsley on top.

Nutrition (per Serving): Calories 112 Carbs 1.2g Protein 8.6g Fat 8.4g

Chocolate Peanut Butter Bars

Prep Time: 15 minutes | Cooking Time: 5 hours

Ingredients (10 Servings):

- 4 oz cream cheese, softened
- 1 large egg, beaten
- 2 cups almond flour
- ½ cup chunky peanut butter
- ½ cup heavy cream
- 2 tbsp stevia sweetener
- 1 tsp vanilla extract
- ½ cup dark chocolate chips

Directions:

Mix the cream cheese, egg, almond flour, peanut butter, heavy cream, stevia, vanilla extract, and chocolate chips in a large mixing bowl using a hand mixer. Put the bottom of the slow cooker with foil and grease with cooking spray. Pour the batter inside the slow cooker and cook for 5 hours or on low or 3 hours on high. Once cooked cut into bars.

Nutrition (per Serving): Calories 350 Carbs 8.4g Protein 14.1g Fat 32.5g

Arugula Cheese Frittata

Prep Time: 15 minutes | Cooking Time: 3 H 10 minutes

Ingredients (6 Servings):

- 6 eggs
- 3/4 cup goat cheese, crumbled
- ½ cup onion, sliced
- 1 1/2 cups red peppers, roasted and chopped
- 3 cups arugula

- 1 tsp oregano, dried
- 1/3 cup almond milk

Directions:

Grease the slow cooker using a cooking spray. Whisk eggs, oregano, and almond milk in a mixing bowl. Arrange red peppers, onion, arugula, and cheese into the slow cooker. Pour egg batter into the slow cooker over the vegetables. Cook on low within 3 hours. Serve hot.

Nutrition (per Serving): Calories 178 Fat 12.8 g Carbs 6 g Protein 11.4 g

Cauliflower Crust Breakfast Pizza

Prep Time: 15 minutes | Cooking Time: 6 hours

Ingredients (4 Servings):

- 3 eggs
- 3 cups riced cauliflower
- 1 cup grated Parmesan cheese
- 8 oz goat cheese, divided
- 1 tbs olive oil
- 1 lemon grated zest

Directions:

Beat eggs, cauliflower, Parmesan cheese, 2 oz of goat cheese until well mixed in a large bowl. Grease the slow cooker using the olive oil. Press the cauliflower batter in an even layer around the cooker's bottom and extend slightly up the sides. Stir the remaining 6 oz of goat cheese and the lemon zest in a small bowl. Dollop spoonsful onto the cauliflower crust, distributing it evenly. Set the lid on the slow cooker, but prop it slightly open with a chopstick or wooden spoon. Cook within 6 hours on low or 3 hours on high, until the edges are slightly browned. Once finished, turn off the cooker but let the pizza sit in it 30 minutes before serving. Serve warm.

Nutrition (per Serving): Calories 332 Fat 24g Carbs 6g Protein 22g

Parmesan Zucchini & Ricotta Frittata

Prep Time: 15 minutes | Cooking Time: 6 hours

Ingredients (6 Servings):

- 10 large eggs
- 2 medium zucchinis, shredded
- 6 oz ricotta cheese
- 10 cherry tomatoes, halved
- 1 tbsp olive oil
- 3 tbsp heavy (whipping) cream
- 3 tbsp finely chopped fresh parsley
- 1 tbsp fresh thyme
- ½ cup grated Parmesan cheese

Directions:

Toss the shredded zucchini with ½ tsp of salt in a colander set in the sink. Let the zucchini sit for a few minutes, then squeeze out the excess liquid with your hands. Grease the slow cooker with olive oil. Beat the eggs, heavy cream, thyme in a large bowl. Put the zucchini and stir. Transfer the mixture to the prepared insert. Using a large spoon, dollop the ricotta cheese into the egg mixture, distributing it evenly. Top with the tomatoes and sprinkle the Parmesan cheese over the top. Set to cook within 6 hours on low or 3 hours on high. Serve at room temperature.

Nutrition (per Serving): Calories 259 Fat 18g Carbs 4g Protein 18g

Cauliflower Hash Browns Breakfast Casserole

Prep Time: 15 minutes | Cooking Time: 5-7 hours

Ingredients (10 Servings):

- 10 eggs
- ½ cup milk
- ½ tsp dry mustard
- 1 head cauliflower, shredded
- 1 small onion, diced
- 5 oz packaged pre-cooked breakfast sausages, sliced
- 5 oz shredded cheddar cheese

Directions:

Grease a slow cooker properly with cooking spray. Mix well eggs, milk, dry mustard. From the shredded cauliflower, take one-third portion and layer it in the bottom of the slow cooker.

After that place one-third of the sliced onion on top. Use pepper and salt to season and top it with one-third portion of sausage and cheese. Repeat the same process by maintaining two layers. Pour the eggs mixture over slow cooker. Cook on low for 5-7 hours and wait until eggs set properly and the top color is browned.

Nutrition (per Serving): Calories 127.7 Fat 9 Carbs 2.2g Protein 8g

Breakfast Casserole

Prep Time: 15-20 minutes | Cooking Time: 12 hours

Ingredients (10 Servings):

- 4 cups daikon radish
- 12 oz cooked, crumbled bacon slices
- 1 lb. cooked grounded sausage
- 1 onion, chopped
- 1 green bell pepper, sliced

- 1 ½ cups mushroom, sliced
- 1 ½ cups fresh spinach
- 2 cups shredded cheese (Monterrey Jack is preferred)
- ½ cup feta cheese, shredded
- 10 eggs
- 1 cup heavy white cream

Directions:

Put a layer of hashed browns in the bottom of the cooker with low flame.

Then put the layer of bacon and sausage over it. Put all the spices upon the layer. Now take a bowl and whisk the eggs and cream and pour the mixture in the cooker. Cover it and let it cook for 6 hours on high flame or for 12 hours on low flame. Then serve.

Nutrition (per Serving): Calories 553 Carbs 5 g Fat 44g Protein 30 g

Bacon-Mushroom Breakfast

Prep Time: 15 minutes | Cooking Time: 4 hours

Ingredients (4 Servings):

- 3½ oz bacon large, sliced
- 2½ oz white mushrooms, chopped
- 5 eggs
- ¼ cup shallots, chopped
- ¾ cup bell pepper, chopped
- 6 kale leaves large, shredded
- 1 cup Parmesan cheese

Directions:

Clean the kale leaves, remove the hard stems and chop into small pieces. In a skillet cook the bacon, till it becomes crispy and add mushrooms, red pepper, and shallot. Add kale and cut down the flame and let the kale become tender in the skillet. Now take a medium bowl and beat all eggs. In the slow cooker, add ghee and let it become hot. Spread the ghee on all side of the cooker. Put the

sautéed vegetable into the base of the cooker. Spread the cheese over the vegetables. Then, add the beaten eggs on top. Just stir it gently. Set the cooker on low heat and cook for about 4 hours.

Serve hot with sliced avocado(optional).

Nutrition (per Serving): Calories 313 Carbs 4g Protein 22.9g Fat 22.2g

Keto Sausage & Egg

Prep Time: 15-20 minutes | Cooking Time: 4-5 hours

Ingredients (6 Servings):

- 10 large eggs
- 10 oz pork sausage links, cooked and sliced
- 1 broccoli, finely chopped
- 1 cup cheddar shredded
- ¾ cup whipping cream
- 2 garlic cloves, minced

Directions:

Take a slow cooker and grease its interior. Put one layer of broccoli, half portion of the cheese and half part of sausage into it. Repeat the layering and put all the ingredients in the cooker. Take a large bowl, and mix eggs, garlic, whipping cream, pepper and salt thoroughly. Transfer the mix over the layered ingredients in the cooker. Cover and cook for about 5 hours. Make sure the edges are not overcooked. Check the center with a toothpick.

Nutrition (per Serving): Calories 384 Fat 38.86 g Carbs 6 g Protein 26.13 g

Egg & Mushroom Breakfast

Prep Time: 15 minutes | Cooking Time: 6 hours

Ingredients (4 Servings):

- 1 cup mushrooms, chopped
- 3 large slices of bacon
- 6 eggs
- 3 tbsp shallots, chopped
- ½ cup bell pepper, red
- 8 large kale leaves, shredded
- 1 cup Parmesan cheese, shredded
- 1 tbsp butter or ghee
- spinach - for dressing
- avocado, sliced - for dressing
- extra virgin olive oil - for dressing

Directions:

Wash, clean and remove the stem of the kale and chop it nicely. Take a pan and cook bacon until it becomes crispy. Add mushroom, pepper, and shallot and continue heating until it becomes soft. Now add kale and switch off the stove and let the kale wilt. Take a small mixing bowl and beat the eggs, with pepper and salt. Grease the inside of the cooker properly and the put the sautéed vegetables in it. Spread the cheese over it. Add the beaten egg on top of the mixture. Stir well and slow heat about 6 hours. You may occasionally check the food after 4 hours. Serve it with sliced avocado, spread with spinach dressed in olive oil.

Nutrition (per Serving): Calories 262 Carbs 6.1 g Fat 16.2 g Protein 22.9 g

Spinach & Ham Breakfast Casserole

Prep Time: 10 minutes | Cooking Time: 1 H 30 minutes

Ingredients (6 Servings):

- 4 large eggs
- ¼ cup milk
- ½ cup greek yogurt
- ½ tsp thyme
- ½ tsp onion powder
- ½ tsp garlic powder
- ⅓ cup diced mushrooms
- 1 cup baby spinach (packed)
- 1 cup shredded pepper jack cheese
- 1 cup ham, diced

Directions:

Mix eggs, milk, yogurt, thyme, onion powder, garlic powder properly in a bowl.

Add mushrooms, spinach, cheese, ham, and stir. Now take a 6-quart slow cooker and spray with non-stick cooking spray. Pour eggs mixture into the cooker and put on slow. Cover and cook on high for 90-120 minutes until eggs appropriately set. Slice and serve for breakfast or dinner.

Nutrition (per Serving): Calories 155.6 Fat 8.7 g Carbs 2.5 g Protein15.6 g

Keto Soup with Miso

Prep Time: 15 minutes | Cooking Time: 8 hours

Ingredients (4 Servings):

- 1 cup pumpkin, diced
- 1 cup broccoli flowerets
- 1 cup zucchini, chopped
- 1 onion chopped
- 2 tbsp miso white
- 4 tbsp olive oil
- 1 garlic clove, minced
- 2 stalks celery stalks, cut into pieces

Directions:

Take a slow cooker and put 2 tbsp olive oil and keep aside. Then take a large skillet, put 2 tbsp of oil and heat it. Add onion, garlic, pumpkin, celery to the heating skillet by sprinkling bit of salt. Sauté for 5 minutes. Transfer this mixture into the slow cooker and put all other ingredients. Now pour about 4 cups of water and salt to taste. Stir well. Take 3 tbsp of water and mix the Miso and add to the slow cooker. Cook for about 8 hours. Serve warm.

Nutrition (per Serving): Calories 95 Carbs 6 g Fat 9 g Fiber 3 g Protein 4 g

Slow cooker Pumpkin Coconut Breakfast Bars

Prep Time: 20 minutes | Cooking Time: 3 hours

Ingredients (8 Servings):

- 1 can puree pumpkin
- 1 tbsp of raw apple cider vinegar
- 2 eggs, beaten
- 1 cup coconut flour
- 1 tsp cinnamon powder
- 1 tsp baking soda
- 1/3 cup pecan, toasted and chopped

Directions:

Use a parchment paper lightly oiled with cooking oil. Mix the pumpkin puree, apple cider vinegar, and eggs. Differently mix the salt, pumpkin pie spice, coconut flour, baking soda, and cinnamon. Pour the wet ingredients to the dry ingredients and mix. Pour the batter into the Slow cooker and sprinkle with pecans. Cover with lid. Cook for 3 hours on low or until a toothpick inserted in the middle comes out clean.

Nutrition (per Serving):   Calories 137.4 Carbs 8.5g Protein 4g Fat 5.2g

Overnight Eggs Benedict Casserole

Prep Time: 25 minutes | Cooking Time: 3 hours

Ingredients (6 Servings):

- 2 bacon slices
- 1 cup milk
- 2 large eggs, beaten
- 6 egg yolks
- 2 tbsp chives, chopped

- 1 ½ sticks butter, cubed

Directions:

Spray cooking oil inside the slow cooker. Put the bacon slices at the bottom of it. Mix the eggs and milk. Season with pepper and salt. Pour over the bacon. Close the lid and cook for 1 ½ hours. Open the lid and add the egg yolks on top. Sprinkle with chopped chives. Continue cooking for another 1 ½ hours or until the egg mixture is done. While still warm, keep butter on top.

Nutrition (per Serving): Calories 126 Carbs 2g Protein 6.2g Fat 8g

Vanilla Pumpkin Bread

Prep Time: 10 minutes | Cooking Time: 2 hours

Ingredients (2 Servings):

- cooking spray
- ½ cup white flour
- ½ cup whole wheat flour
- ½ tsp baking soda
- A pinch of cinnamon powder
- 2 tbsp olive oil
- 2 tbsp maple syrup
- 1 egg
- ½ tbsp milk
- ½ tsp vanilla extract
- ½ cup pumpkin puree
- 2 tbsp walnuts, chopped
- 2 tbsp chocolate chips

Directions:

In a bowl, mix white flour with whole wheat flour, baking soda, cinnamon and stir.

Add maple syrup, olive oil, egg, milk, vanilla extract, pumpkin puree, walnuts and chocolate chips and stir well. Grease a loaf pan that fits your slow cooker with cooking spray, pour pumpkin bread, transfer to your cooker and cook on High for 2 hours. Slice bread, divide between plates and serve.

Nutrition (per Serving): Calories 340 Fat 13g Fiber 5g Carbs 48g Protein 10g

Almond Banana Bread

Prep Time: 10 minutes | Cooking Time: 4 hours

Ingredients (2 Servings):

- 1 egg
- 2 tbsp butter, melted
- ½ cup sugar
- 1 cup flour
- ½ tsp baking powder
- ¼ tsp baking soda
- a pinch of cinnamon powder
- a pinch of nutmeg, ground
- 2 bananas, mashed
- ¼ cup almonds, sliced
- cooking spray

Directions:

In a bowl, mix sugar with flour, baking powder, baking soda, cinnamon, nutmeg and stir. Add egg, butter, almonds, bananas and stir really well. Grease your slow cooker with cooking spray, pour bread mix; cover and cook on Low for 4 hours. Slice bread and serve for breakfast.

Nutrition (per Serving): Calories 454 Fat 10g Carbs 76g Protein 15g

Sage Potato Casserole

Prep Time: 10 minutes | Cooking Time: 3 hours

Ingredients (2 Servings):

- 1 tsp onion powder
- 3 eggs, whisked

- ½ tsp garlic powder
- ½ tsp sage, dried
- ½ yellow onion, chopped
- 1 tbsp parsley, chopped
- 2 garlic cloves, minced
- a pinch of red pepper flakes
- ½ tbsp olive oil
- 2 red potatoes, cubed

Directions:

Grease your slow cooker with the oil, add potatoes, onion, garlic, parsley and pepper flakes and toss a bit. In a bowl, mix eggs with onion powder, garlic powder, sage, salt and pepper, whisk well and pour over potatoes. Cover, cook on High for 3 hours and 30 minutes, divide into 2 plates and serve for breakfast.

Nutrition (per Serving): Calories 298 Fat 11g Carbs 34g Protein 15g

Pear & Maple Oatmeal

Prep Time: 10 minutes | Cooking Time: 4 hours

Ingredients (2 Servings):

- 1 ½ cups milk
- ½ cup steel cut oats
- ½ tsp vanilla extract
- 1 pear, chopped
- ½ tsp maple extract
- 1 tbsp sugar

Directions:

In your slow cooker, combine milk with oats, vanilla, pear, maple extract and sugar, stir, cover and cook on Low for 4 hours. Divide into bowls and serve for breakfast.

Nutrition (per Serving): Calories 110 Fat 5g Fiber 7g Carbs 18g Protein 4g

Almond & Strawberry Oatmeal

Prep Time: 10 minutes | Cooking Time: 6 hours

Ingredients (3 Servings):

- 1 cup steel cut oats
- 3 cups water
- 1 cup almond milk
- 1 cup strawberries, chopped
- ½ cup Greek yogurt
- ½ tsp cinnamon powder
- ½ tsp vanilla extract

Directions:

In your slow cooker, mix oats with water, milk, strawberries, yogurt, cinnamon and vanilla. Toss, cover and cook on Low for 6 hours. Stir your oatmeal one more time, divide into bowls and serve for breakfast.

Nutrition (per Serving): Calories 236 Fat 7g Carbs 34g Protein 7g

Cheddar Sausage Potatoes

Prep Time: 10 minutes | Cooking Time: 4 hours

Ingredients (4 Servings):

- 2 potatoes, chopped
- ½ red bell pepper, chopped
- ½ green bell pepper, chopped
- ½ yellow onion, chopped
- 4 oz smoked Italian sausage, sliced
- 1 cup cheddar cheese, shredded
- ¼ cup sour cream
- A pinch of oregano, dried
- ¼ tsp basil, dried
- 4 oz chicken cream
- 1 tbsp parsley, chopped

Directions:

Put the potato in your slow cooker, add red bell pepper, green bell pepper, onion, sausage, cheese, sour cream, oregano, basil, and chicken cream, cover and cook on Low for 4 hours. Add parsley, toss, divide between plates and serve for breakfast.

Nutrition (per Serving): Calories 325 Fat 15g Fiber 4g Carbs 20g Protein 12g

Coconut Berries Quinoa Mix

Prep Time: 10 minutes | Cooking Time: 8 hours

Ingredients (2 Servings):

- ½ cup quinoa
- 1 cup water
- ½ cup coconut milk
- 1 tbsp maple syrup
- 1 tbsp mix berries

Directions:

In your slow cooker, mix quinoa with water, coconut milk, maple syrup and salt. Stir well, cover and cook on Low for 8 hours. Divide into 2 bowls, sprinkle berries on top and serve for breakfast.

Nutrition (per Serving): Calories 225 Fat 15g Carbs 22g Protein 5g

Cheddar Hash Browns

Prep Time: 10 minutes | Cooking Time: 3 hours

Ingredients (2 Servings):

- 6 oz hash browns
- ½ cup milk
- 1 tbsp butter
- 2 tbsp mushrooms, chopped
- 2 tbsp yellow onion, chopped
- ¼ tsp garlic powder
- 1 tbsp flour
- ¼ cup sour cream

- ¼ cup cheddar cheese, shredded
- ½ tbsp parsley, chopped
- Cooking spray

Directions:

Heat up a pan with the butter over medium heat; add onion and mushroom, garlic powder and flour, stir and cook for 1 minute. Add milk gradually, stir and cook until it thickens and take off heat. Grease your slow cooker with cooking spray and add mushrooms mix. Add hash browns, sour cream and cheddar cheese. Cover and cook on High for 3 hours. Divide between plates and serve.

Nutrition (per Serving): Calories 334 Fat 24g Carbs 22g Protein 10g

Cheddar & Bacon Casserole

Prep Time: 10 minutes | Cooking Time: 3 hours

Ingredients (2 Servings):

- 6 oz hash browns, shredded
- 2 bacon slices, cooked and chopped
- 2 oz cheddar cheese, shredded
- 4 eggs, whisked
- 1 green onion, chopped
- ¼ cup milk
- cooking spray

Directions:

Grease your slow cooker with cooking spray and add hash browns, bacon and cheese.

In a bowl, mix eggs with green onion, milk, salt and pepper, whisk well and add to slow cooker. Cover, cook on High for 3 hours, divide between plates and serve.

Nutrition (per Serving): Calories 401 Fat 24g Carbs 20g Protein 18g

Cream Cheese Banana Breakfast

Prep Time: 10 minutes | Cooking Time: 4 hours

Ingredients (2 Servings):

- ½ French baguette, sliced
- 2 bananas, sliced
- 2 oz cream cheese
- 1 tbsp brown sugar
- ¼ cup walnuts, chopped
- 1 egg, whisked
- 2 tbsp skim milk
- 2 tbsp honey
- ½ tsp cinnamon powder
- ¼ tsp vanilla extract
- 1 tbsp butter
- cooking spray

Directions:

Spread cream cheese on all bread slices and grease your slow cooker with cooking spray.

Arrange bread slices in your slow cooker, layer banana slices, brown sugar and walnuts.

In a bowl, mix eggs with skim milk, honey, cinnamon, and vanilla extract, and whisk and add over bread slices. Add butter, cover, cook on Low for 4 hours, divide between plates and serve.

Nutrition (per Serving): Calories 346 Fat 22g Carbs 29g Protein 8g

Carrots Zucchini Oatmeal

Prep Time: 10 minutes | Cooking Time: 8 hours

Ingredients (2 Servings):

- ½ cup steel cut oats
- 1 cup coconut milk
- 1 carrot, grated
- ¼ cup zucchini, grated
- A pinch of nutmeg, ground

- ½ tsp cinnamon powder
- 2 tbsp brown sugar
- ¼ cup pecans, chopped
- Cooking spray

Directions:

Grease your slow cooker with cooking spray, add oats, milk, carrot, zucchini, nutmeg, cinnamon and sugar, toss, cover and cook on Low for 8 hours. Divide into 2 bowls, sprinkle pecans on top and serve.

Nutrition (per Serving): Calories 437 Fat 34g Carbs 29g Protein 10g

Tater Tot Casserole

Prep Time: 10 minutes | Cooking Time: 4 hours

Ingredients (2 Servings):

- cooking spray
- 6 oz tater tots, frozen
- 2 eggs, whisked
- ½ lb. turkey sausage, ground
- 1 tbsp heavy cream
- ¼ tsp thyme, dried
- ½ cup Colby jack cheese, shredded

Directions:

Grease your slow cooker with cooking spray, spread tater tots on the bottom, add sausage, thyme, garlic powder, salt, pepper and whisked eggs. Add cheese, cover pot and cook on Low for 4 hours. Divide between plates and serve.

Nutrition (per Serving): Calories 327 Fat 25g Carbs 10g Protein 13g

Banana & Blueberry Oats

Prep Time: 10 minutes | Cooking Time: 6 hours

Ingredients (2 Servings):

- ½ cup steel cut oats
- ¼ cup quinoa
- ½ cup blueberries
- 1 banana, mashed
- a pinch of cinnamon powder
- 2 tbsp maple syrup
- 2 cups water
- cooking spray
- ½ cup coconut milk

Directions:

Grease your slow cooker with cooking spray, add oats, quinoa, blueberries, banana, cinnamon, maple syrup, water and coconut milk, stir, cover and cook on Low for 6 hours. Divide into 2 bowls and serve for breakfast.

Nutrition (per Serving): Calories 529 Fat 28.4g Carbs 62.8g Protein 11g

Peanut Butter Oatmeal

Prep Time: 10 minutes | Cooking Time: 8 hours

Ingredients (2 Servings):

- 1 banana, mashed
- 2 cups almond milk
- ½ cup steel cut oats
- 2 tbsp peanut butter
- ½ tsp cinnamon powder
- ½ tbsp chia seeds

Directions:

In your slow cooker, mix almond milk with banana, oats, peanut butter, cinnamon and chia, stir, cover and cook on Low for 8 hours. Stir oatmeal one more time, divide into 2 bowls and serve.

Nutrition (per Serving): Calories 334 Fat 13g Carbs 45g Protein 11g

Cranberry Apple Oats

Prep Time: 10 minutes | Cooking Time: 3 hours

Ingredients (2 Servings):

- cooking spray
- 2 cups water
- 1 cup old fashioned oats
- ¼ cup cranberries, dried
- 1 apple, chopped
- 1 tbsp butter, melted
- ½ tsp cinnamon powder

Directions:

Grease your slow cooker with cooking spray, add water, oats, cranberries, apple, butter and cinnamon; stir well, cover and cook on Low for 3 hours. Stir oatmeal again, divide into bowls and serve for breakfast.

Nutrition (per Serving): Calories 242 Fat 4g Carbs 38g Protein 10g

SALT & PEPPER *the list of ingredient list do not indicate the amount of salt and pepper: you can add approximately a teaspoon of salt and, in if you like it, 1/2 teaspoon of pepper for each recipe*

CHAPTER 2: SOUPS AND STEWS

Savory Zucchini Stew

Prep Time: 20 minutes | Cooking Time: 6 hours

Ingredients (6 Servings):

- 1 ½ lb. Italian sausage
- 1 cup celery, chopped small
- 3 cups sliced zucchini, sliced into rounds
- 1 green bell pepper, chopped small
- 1 red or yellow bell pepper, chopped
- 1 large onion, diced
- 2 garlic cloves, minced
- 3 cans diced tomatoes
- ½ cup water
- 1 tsp brown sugar
- 2 tsp Italian seasoning
- 1 tsp dried basil
- ¼ cup cheese, grated

Directions:

Fry the sausage on medium heat on the stove. Break up the meat with a spatula and make sure it's fully cooked (5-8 minutes). Drain off the grease. Add the celery, onions and peppers and continue to cook until the vegetables become soft and translucent (7-8 minutes). Add minced garlic, cook and stir continually until fragrant (2 minutes). Stir and remove from the heat.

Pour sausage mixture into the slow cooker. Put the 3 cans of diced tomatoes with spices, sugar, and water. Cook on low for 4-6 hours. Top with grated cheese and add a fresh sprig of basil (optional).

Nutrition (per Serving): Carbs 16g Calories 280 Fat 22g Protein 23g

Creamy Pumpkin Bisque

Prep Time: 15 minutes | Cooking Time: 5 hours

Ingredients (6 Servings):

- 1 pumpkin (butternut, sugar, etc)
- 1 medium sweet potato, peeled and diced
- 2 carrots, chopped
- 1 medium yellow onion, chopped
- 2 cup vegetable stock
- 1 tsp curry powder
- ½ tsp ground ginger
- ½ tsp ground nutmeg
- 1 cup heavy cream

Directions:

Peel pumpkin skin and remove pulp and seeds. Cube up the pumpkin flesh. Place pumpkin, potato, carrots, onion, vegetable stock, and spices in the slow cooker. Cook within 4-5 hours, low or 2-3 hours, high. Make sure vegetables are incredibly tender. Pulse in a blender, then return it inside the slow cooker and add in the heavy cream, stirring until thoroughly mixed. Heat back up to desired heat and serve.

Nutrition (per Serving): Carbs 13g Calories 175, Fat 15g, Protein 2g

Zesty White Chicken Chili

Prep Time: 15 minutes | Cooking Time: 8 hours

Ingredients (6 Servings):

- 2 lb. boneless, skinless chicken breasts or thighs
- 1 yellow onion, diced
- 1 medium green bell pepper, chopped
- 1 small jalapeno, minced
- 6 garlic cloves, minced
- 3 tsp ground cumin (add more to taste)
- 1 tsp dried oregano
- 6 cups chicken stock
- 1 lime, juiced
- ½ cup fresh cilantro, chopped

Directions:

Throw the peppers, jalapeno, onion, garlic, spices into the slow cooker. Place the chicken on top and fill with broth. Cook covered on low for 7-8 hours. Check the chicken with a fork to see if it is falling apart. Add the lime juice and stir. When serving, top off with cilantro.

Nutrition (per Serving): Carbs 6g Calories 105 Fat 0g Protein 25 g

Beef Stew

Prep Time: 15 minutes | Cooking Time: 7 hours

Ingredients (6 Servings):

- 2 lb. stewing beef, diced into 1-inch cubes
- 2 tbsp olive oil
- 3 large carrots (4-5 medium/small), chopped
- 2 large yellow onions, diced
- 2 large stalks of celery, chopped
- 3 garlic cloves, minced
- ¼ cup all-purpose flour
- 2 cups beef broth
- ¼ cup Dijon mustard
- 1 tbsp brown sugar
- 1 tbsp rosemary
- 1 tsp dried thyme

Directions:

Massage the beef with salt plus pepper and coat all sides with the flour. Heat-up the oil in a large skillet over medium heat, then put onions and garlic and sauté for 1-2 minutes. Add the flower-coated beef to the skillet and sear on all sides for 2-3 minutes.

Place the beef, onions and garlic into the slow cooker and add the carrots. Put the skillet with the beef drippings back on the burner and add all the rest of the ingredients to the hot skillet. Stir the mixture, and make sure to stir up any beef or garlic remnants at the bottom of the pan. Heat-up, then stir until the sugar has dissolved the mixture is well-combined. Pour the broth mixture over the beef and carrots in the slow cooker—Cook within 7-8 hours, low or high for 4 hours. Keep warm until you're ready to serve it. Garnish with fresh parsley if desired.

Nutrition (per Serving): Carbs 11g Calories 250 Fat 12g Protein 20g

Lamb and Rosemary Stew

Prep Time: 15 minutes | Cooking Time: 8 hours

Ingredients (4 Servings):

- 1 ½ lb. lamb, cut into cubes
- 1 onion, roughly chopped
- 2 garlic cloves, finely chopped
- 1 lamb stock cube
- 3 tbsp olive oil
- 2 cup water

Directions:

Add olive oil into the Slow cooker. Brown the lamb in an oiled skillet for 2 minutes. Add 2 cups of water, stock cube, garlic, onion, lamb to the pot. Cook on low within 8 hours. Serve.

Nutrition (per Serving): Calories 298 Fat 18.3g Carbs 3.9g Protein 30.6g

Lamb and Eggplant Stew

Prep Time: 15 minutes | Cooking Time: 8 H 30 minutes

Ingredients (4 Servings):

- 2 lb. minced lamb
- 1 onion, finely chopped
- 2 garlic cloves, crushed
- 1 eggplant, cut into small cubes
- 2 tomatoes, chopped
- 1 stock cube
- ¾ cup grated mozzarella
- 2 tbsp olive oil
- 2 cups water

Directions:

Add olive oil into the Slow cooker. Add water, lamb, onion, garlic, eggplant, stock cube, tomatoes, rosemary, salt, and pepper to the pot. Stir to mix. Cook within 8 hours, high. Remove the lid and stir the stew. Sprinkle the mozzarella on top, cover with the lid, and cook 30 minutes more. Serve.

Nutrition (per Serving): Calories 432 Fat 21g Carbs 8.8g Protein 50.9g

Bacon and Cauliflower Soup

Prep Time: 15 minutes | Cooking Time: 4 hours

Ingredients (4 Servings):

- 1 large cauliflower cut into chunks
- 2 garlic cloves, crushed
- 1 onion, finely chopped
- 4 bacon slices, cut into small pieces
- 2 cups chicken stock
- 1 tsp paprika
- ½ tsp chili powder
- ½ cup heavy cream
- 2 tbsp olive oil

Directions:

Add olive oil into the Slow cooker. Add the garlic, cauliflower, onion, bacon, stock, paprika, chili, salt, and pepper to the pot. Stir to mix. Cook on high within 4 hours. Open the lid and blend with a hand mixer. Add the cream and mix. Serve sprinkled with paprika.

Nutrition (per Serving): Calories 205 Fat 22.3g Carbs 6.1g Protein 10.4g

Pot Roast Soup

Prep Time: 15 minutes | Cooking Time: 8 hours

Ingredients (4 Servings):

- ½ diced butternut squash
- 1 cup chicken stock
- 1 diced onion
- 1 can diced tomatoes
- 1 ¼ lb. stew meat
- 3 diced carrots
- 7 oz mushrooms, diced
- 1 tsp cumin, basil and oregano

Directions:

Arrange the vegetables in layers at the bottom of the slow cooker. Pour in the stew meat, then sprinkle in the spices as desired, then stir to combine. Cook for 5 hours on high or for 8 hours on low. Then serve.

Nutrition (per Serving): Calories 227 Carbs 10 g Fat 12g Protein 20g

Chicken with Kale Leaves Soup

Prep Time: 15 minutes | Cooking Time: 6 hours

Ingredients (6 Servings):

- 2 lb. chicken breast
- 1/3 cup lime juice
- 1/3 cup onion finely chopped
- 3 tbsp olive oil
- 4 oz baby kale leaves
- 10 oz chicken broth

Directions:

Using a large skillet, add in a tbsp of oil and heat over medium heat. Cook the chicken for 15 minutes. Once done, shred the chicken then transfer it into the slow cooker. Pour the onions, chicken broth, and olive oil into a food processor and blend until well combined. Pour the broth mix into the slow cooker, then add in the rest of the ingredients and stir. Cover the pot then cook for 6 hours on low settings, occasionally stirring. Serve.

Nutrition (per Serving): Calories 150 Carbs 5g Fat 9g Protein 27g

Southern Paleo Slow cooker Chili

Prep Time: 10 minutes | Cooking Time: 8 hours

Ingredients (4 Servings):

- 1 lb. beef
- 20 oz tomatoes, chopped
- 3 chopped carrots

- 1 tsp onion powder
- 1 tsp paprika
- 1 diced onion
- 1 tsp garlic powder
- 1 tbsp Worcestershire sauce
- 1 tbsp fresh parsley, chopped
- 1 seeded & diced green bell pepper
- 3 tsp chili powder

Directions:

Using a medium-sized skillet, add in the ground beef and brown over high heat, occasionally stirring until there is no pink. Put the browned beef inside the slow cooker, including the fat.

Add onion, green bell pepper, tomatoes, and carrots into the slow cooker. Mix all the fixing, then put in all the remaining seasonings and spices. Stir all the ingredients together again, then cover and cook for 8 hours on low settings or 5 on high settings. Serve then top with sour cream and jalapenos and enjoy.

Nutrition (per Serving): Calories 211 Carbs 6g Fat 12g Protein 20g

Dairy-Free Chili Chicken Soup

Prep Time: 30 minutes | Cooking Time: 6 hours

Ingredients (10 Servings):

- 2 lb. boneless chicken thighs
- 1 cup coconut milk
- 1 tsp chili powder
- 1 yellow onion diced
- 1 tbsp minced garlic
- 2 tsp cumin
- 2 cups chicken broth
- 2 (8 oz) cans green chilies, diced
- 2 cans beans
- ¼ cup arrowroot starch
- ½ cup water

Directions:

Put all the items into the slow cooker, then cover and cook for 5-6 hours on high settings.

Remove the chicken from the slow cooker, then transfer into a medium-sized bowl, then shred.

Take the chicken back inside the slow cooker, then stir until properly distributed, then allow to cook for an extra 30 minutes. Taste for seasoning as desired. Serve then garnish with any toppings of your choice and enjoy.

Nutrition (per Serving): Calories 331 Carbs 12g Fat 17g Protein 27 g

Low Carbohydrate Slow cooker Soup

Prep Time: 15 minutes | Cooking Time: 4 hours

Ingredients (8 Servings):

- 2 lb. ground pork beef
- 8 oz cream cheese
- 3 cups chicken broth
- ½ cup shredded cheese, to garnish
- 2 tbsp fresh cilantro
- 2 tbsp taco seasonings
- 2 diced tomato cans

Directions:

Cook the ground pork beef over medium-high heat in a large skillet. In the meantime, place the diced tomatoes, cream cheese, and taco seasoning into the slow cooker. Drain the meat of the grease and transfer it into the slow cooker. Mix the ingredients, then add the chicken broth over the meat. Cover the chicken then cook for 4 hours on low or 2 hours on high settings.

Stir in the cilantro before serving. Serve the garnish with the shredded cheese.

Nutrition (per Serving): Calories 291 Carbs 11g Fat 19g Protein 27g

Slow cooker Cheeseburger Soup

Prep Time: 15 minutes | Cooking Time: 6 hours

Ingredients (5 Servings):

- 2 lb. ground beef
- 2 bacon slices
- ½ cup cheese
- ½ cup chopped onions
- ½ chopped red bell pepper
- 1 tsp garlic powder
- 1 tsp Worcestershire sauce
- 2 chopped tomatoes
- 3 cups beef broth
- 3 chopped celery sticks
- 6 oz tomato paste

Directions:

Using a large saucepan, add in the ground beef and brown. Halfway through the browning process, drain off every fat, add in the red pepper, onions, celery, and continue cooking.

Add the remaining ingredients and beef mixture into the slow cooker then stir to combine.

If desired, add in more beef broth, cover, and cook for 6 hours on low setting or 3 hours on a high setting, occasionally stirring. Serve then top with a full spoon of cheese and bacon slices (if desired), then enjoy.

Nutrition (per Serving): Calories 380 Carbs 14g Fat 23g Protein 37g

Delicious Kernel Corn Taco Soup

Prep Time: 10 minutes | Cooking Time: 8 hours

Ingredients (6 Servings):

- 1 lb. ground beef
- 1 can whole kernel corn, with liquid
- 1 ½ onion, chopped
- 1 package taco seasoning mix
- 1 can dice green chili peppers
- 1 can tomato sauce
- 2 cans peeled and diced tomatoes
- 1 can chili beans, with liquid
- 2 cups of water
- 1 can kidney beans with liquid

Directions:

Sauté your beef in a skillet until it is brown on all sides and keep aside.

Put your browned beef into your slow cooker and add all other ingredients and toss together to blend evenly. Cook within 8 hours, low.

Nutrition (per Serving): Calories 263 Carbs 34g Fat 8g Protein 15g

Ham and Lentil Consommé

Prep Time: 15 minutes | Cooking Time: 8 hours

Ingredients (6 Servings):

- 1 ½ cups diced cooked ham
- 8 tsp tomato sauce
- 1 cup onion, diced
- 1 cup dried lentils
- 1 cup of water
- 1 cup celery, chopped
- ½ tsp dried basil
- 32 oz chicken broth
- 1 cup carrots, diced
- ¼ tsp dried thyme
- 2 cloves garlic, minced
- ½ tsp dried oregano
- 1 bay leaf

Directions:

Put all your fixing into your slow cooker and mix very well to blend well.

Cook within 8 hours, low heat settings. Remove your bay leaf before serving it.

Nutrition (per Serving): Calories 194 Carbs 15g Fat 8g Protein 40g

Beef Barley Vegetable Soup

Prep Time: 15 minutes | Cooking Time: 8 hours

Ingredients (10 Servings):

- 1 package frozen mixed vegetables
- 1 beef chuck roast
- 1 onion, chopped
- ½ cup barley
- 4 cups of water
- 1 can chop stewed tomatoes
- 1 bay leaf
- 3 stalks celery, chopped
- 3 carrots, chopped
- 4 cubes beef bouillon cube
- 2 tbsp oil
- 1 tbsp white sugar

Directions:

Season your beef with salt, adding bay leaf and barley in the last hour; cook your beef in your slow cooker for 8 hours or until tender. Set your beef aside; keep your broth also aside.

Stir fry your onion, celery, carrots, and frozen vegetable mix until soft. Add your bouillon cubes, pepper, water, salt, beef mixture, barley mixture, chopped stewed tomatoes, and broth. Bring to boiling point and simmer at lowered heat for 20 minutes.

Nutrition (per Serving): Calories 99 Carbs 15g Fat 2g Protein 5g

Chicken Soup with Lemongrass

Prep Time: 5 minutes | Cooking Time: 8 hours

Ingredients (10 Servings):

- 1 whole chicken
- 1 stalk of lemongrass, cut into big hunks
- 5 thick slices of fresh ginger
- 20 fresh basil leaves (10 -slow cooker; 10 -spices)
- 1 lime

Directions:

Put your lemongrass, ginger, 10 basil leaves, and chicken into the slow cooker. Fill the slow cooker up with water. Boil the chicken mixture for 8 - 10 hours. Scoop the soup into a bowl and adjust your salt to taste. Juice in the lime to taste and spice up with the chopped basil leaves.

Nutrition (per Serving): Calories 185 Carbs 1g Fat 8g Protein 29g

Slow cooker Pork Stew with Tapioca

Prep Time: 15 minutes | Cooking Time: 10 hours

Ingredients (6 Servings):

- 3 tbsp quick-cooking tapioca
- 1 tbsp vegetable oil
- 1 large onion, chopped
- 1 ½ lb. pork stew meat, cut into bite-size pieces
- 2 tsp Worcestershire sauce
- 1 stalk celery, chopped
- 4 carrots, sliced
- 1 tbsp beef bouillon granules
- 3 red potatoes, cubes
- 3 cups vegetable juice

Directions:

Heat your oil over medium-high heat and brown your beef on all sides.

Mix your browned beef with all other ingredients in the slow cooker. Cover and cook on low heat settings for 9-10 hours.

Nutrition (per Serving): Calories 240 Carbs 16g Fat 10g Protein 25g

Delicious Bacon Cheese Potato Soup

Prep Time: 15 minutes | Cooking Time: 10 hours

Ingredients (8 Servings):

- 3 lb. large baking potatoes, peeled, cut into 1/2-inch cubes
- ¼ cup chopped fresh chives
- 8 slices bacon, diced
- 1 carton chicken broth, divided
- ½ cup milk
- 1 onion, finely chopped
- 1 pkg. Shredded Triple Cheddar Cheese, divided
- ½ cup Sour Cream
- 2 tbsp flour

Directions:

Stir fry bacon over medium heat in a large skillet. Remove bacon with your slotted spoon and leave the drippings in the skillet. Stir fry your onions in the skillet for few minutes until it is soft and crisp. Add in your flour and cook for 1 minute, stirring it frequently. Add 1 cup of your chicken broth and cook for 2-3 minutes or until sauce is thick and simmers. Pour the sauce into your slow cooker. Add your remaining chicken broth and potatoes and cook with slow cooker cover for 8-10 hours on low heat settings. Transfer 4 cups of your potatoes in a bowl and mash it until smooth, adding 1.5 cups of cheese to the remaining mixture in the slow cooker; stir until melted. Stir your mashed potatoes into the slow cooker with milk added and cook again within 5 minutes with the lid.

Microwave your bacon in a microwavable plate within 30 seconds or until heated. Serve your soup with bacon, using sour cream, chives, and remaining cheese as toppings.

Nutrition (per Serving): Calories 330 Carbs 48g Fat 11g Protein 6g

Tasty Tomato Soup with Parmesan

Prep Time: 15 minutes | Cooking Time: 3 hours

Ingredients (6 Servings):

- 28 oz of tomatoes, chopped
- ½ cup heavy cream
- ½ cup grated Parmesan cheese
- 10-12 large basil leaves
- 3 tbsp chopped garlic
- ½ tbsp dried thyme
- ¼ tsp of red pepper flakes
- 1 tbsp onion powder

Directions:

Add all ingredients except parmesan and heavy cream to your slow cooker and cook on high heat for 3 hours. Add your cheese and cream and stir. Adjust seasoning to taste. Serve.

Nutrition (per Serving): Calories 300 Carbs 46g Fat 9g Protein 6g

Luscious Carrot Beef Stew with Potatoes

Prep Time: 15 minutes | Cooking Time: 10 hours

Ingredients (8 Servings):

- 2 lb. beef stew meat, bite-sized
- 32 oz beef broth
- 1 tsp oregano
- 2 cups baby carrots
- 2 celery ribs, chopped

- 1 tbsp dried parsley
- ¼ cup of water
- 1 cup of frozen corn
- 2 tbsp Worcestershire sauce
- 2-3 cloves of garlic, grated
- ¼ cup flour
- 6oz can tomato paste
- 4-5 red potatoes, bite-sized
- 1 cup frozen pea
- 1 medium onion, finely chopped

Directions:

Add your tomato paste, beef, beef broth, celery, Worcestershire sauce, carrots, oregano, red onions, parsley, potatoes, garlic, salt, and pepper into your slow cooker and mix.

Cook on low heat for 10 hours. Mix the flour plus water in a small bowl and pour it into your slow cooker 30 minutes before serving and mix until well combined. Stir in your corn and frozen peas and cook for another 30 minutes in the slow cooker, covered. Then serve.

Nutrition (per Serving): Calories 329 Carbs 26g Fat 14g Protein 20g

Delicious Lasagna Consommé

Prep Time: 15 minutes | Cooking Time: 7 hours

Ingredients (8 Servings):

- 1 lb. ground beef
- 2 cups uncooked shell pasta
- 1 tbsp dried parsley
- 1 can of diced tomatoes
- 1 cup of water
- 3 cups of beef broth
- 1 tbsp dried basil
- ½ cup chopped onion
- 1 cup vegetable stock
- 4-5 cloves of garlic, grated
- 1, 6oz can of tomato paste

- Shredded cheese- topping

Directions:

Mix tomato paste and can tomatoes in your slow cooker. Add garlic, salt, broth, stock, pepper, basil, beef, and parsley. Mix, then cook on low heat for 7 hours. Precisely 30 minutes left of cooking time, add 1 cup of water and noodles into your slow cooker. Stir together and cook with the lid back on for 30 minutes.

Nutrition (per Serving): Calories 268 Carbs 25g Fat 10g Protein 12g

Cheese Broccoli Potato Bouillabaisse

Prep Time: 15 minutes | Cooking Time: 8 hours

Ingredients (8 Servings):

- 1 tbsp butter
- 1 ½ lb. potatoes, chopped into 3/4 in cubes
- 2 ½ cups boiling water
- 1 cup onion, sliced
- 1 package frozen broccoli, chopped
- 1 package cheddar cheese, minced
- 2 chicken bouillon cubes

Directions:

Butter the saucepan and fry your onions until crisp. Add your water, bouillon cubes, sautéed onions, and potatoes into a pot and cover it up. Cook under medium heat until potatoes are soft. Place your cheddar cheese and broccoli in your slow cooker while you cook your potatoes. Melt and defrost your cheese and broccoli on low heat settings. Blend your soft potatoes contents using a food processor to your desired consistency and pour it into your slow cooker.

Heat up on low heat settings until it is warm.

Nutrition (per Serving): Calories 100 Carbs 15g Fat 2g Protein 5g

Chicken Thigh & Breast Low Carb Soup

Prep Time: 5 minutes | Cooking Time: 6 hours

Ingredients (6 Servings):

- 2 skin on & bone chicken thighs
- 2 skin on & bone-in chicken breasts
- 1 chopped medium onion
- 1 tsp apple cider vinegar
- 1 tbsp herbs de Provence
- 3 diced carrots
- 3 diced celery stalks
- 3-4 cups filtered water

Directions:

Place the ingredients in layers inside the slow cooker. Make sure the bone side of the chicken is down on top of the veggies. Add in surplus water until the veggies are submerged, and the chicken is covered halfway. Cover the slow cooker then cook for 6-8 hours. Remove the chicken from the slow cooker one done and cool, then remove the bones and skin. Shred the chicken, then return into the slow cooker, season to taste, reheat, then serve and enjoy.

Nutrition (per Serving): Calories 97 Carbs 6g Fat 2g Protein 14g

Beef & Pumpkin Stew

Prep Time: 5 minutes | Cooking Time: 4 hours

Ingredients (4 Servings):

- 2 cup pumpkin
- ½ lb. stewing steak
- 1 tsp sage
- 1 tsp mixed herbs
- 2 tbsp rosemary
- 2 tbsp thyme

- 6 tbsp coconut oil

Directions:

Trim off every excess fat from the stewing steak then transfer it into the slow cooker.

Season the steak with half of the coconut oil then and in salt & pepper. Cover the slow cooker then cook on high setting for 1 hour. Remove the steak from the slow cooker to a serving platter alongside all the remaining seasoning and coconut oil. Mix everything, then transfer back into the slow cooker with the pumpkin and cook for 3 hours on a low setting. Serve with the fresh mixed herbs.

Nutrition (per Serving): Calories 104 Carbs 3g Fat 7g Protein 9g

Jalapeno Low Carb Soup

Prep Time: 10 minutes | Cooking Time: 7 hours

Ingredients (8 Servings):

- 2 seeded & chopped jalapenos
- 1 ½ lb. chicken breasts, boneless
- ¼ tsp paprika
- ½ chopped onion
- ½ chopped green pepper
- ½ cup heavy whipping cream
- ½ lb. cooked & crumbled bacon
- ¾ cup cheddar Cheese
- ¾ cup Monterrey Jack Cheese
- 1 tsp cumin
- 2 minced garlic cloves
- 3 tbsp butter
- 3 cups chicken broth
- 6 oz cream cheese

Directions:

Dissolve the butter, then cook the green peppers, seasoning, jalapenos, and onions until translucent in a medium-sized pan. Scoop the mixture into the slow cooker, then add in the chicken broth and breast. Cover the slow cooker then cook for 3-4 hours on high or 6-7 hours on a low setting. Separate the chicken, and shred it, then return it into the slow cooker.

Put in the heavy whipping cream, cream cheese, remaining cheeses, bacon then stir until the cheese melts. Serve, then top with cheddar cheese, bacon, or jalapenos and enjoy.

Nutrition (per Serving): Calories 540 Carbs 3g Fat 37g Protein 43g

Lean Beef & Mixed Veggies Soup

Prep Time: 8 minutes | Cooking Time: 6 hours

Ingredients (6 Servings):

- 1 ½ lb. beef stew meat
- ½ tsp garlic salt, if desired
- 1 peeled small onion
- 1 diced small green pepper
- 1 tsp garlic & herb seasoning
- 1 small zucchini, sliced into rounds
- 1 can rinse & drained cannellini beans
- 1 small yellow squash, sliced into rounds
- 1 can diced roasted tomatoes
- 1-3 bay leaves
- 2 cups of frozen mixed vegetables
- 4 cups low salt beef broth
- 4 peeled & chopped garlic cloves

Directions:

Add all the ingredients except the zucchini and cannellini beans, mixed vegetables, and yellow squash into the slow cooker. Cover the pot then cook on high for 4 hours. After 4 hours, add in the zucchini, cannellini beans, yellow squash, and mixed vegetables.

Season to taste and cook for an extra 2 hours on high. Once done, stir then serve and enjoy.

Nutrition (per Serving): Calories 336 Carbs 14g Fat 12g Protein 20g

Chicken & Tortilla Soup

Prep Time: 7 minutes | Cooking Time: 2 H 10 minutes

Ingredients (6 Servings):

- 1 diced sweet onion
- 1 tsp cumin
- 1 tsp chili powder
- 1 neatly chopped cilantro bunch
- 1 can diced tomatoes
- 1-2 cups water
- 2 cups celery, chopped
- 2 cups carrots, shredded
- 2 tbsp tomato paste
- 2 diced & de-seeded jalapenos
- 2 big skinned chicken breasts, sliced into 1/2" strips
- 4 minced garlic cloves
- 32 oz organic chicken broth
- olive oil

Directions:

Pour a dash of olive oil, 1/4 cup of chicken broth, the garlic, onions, pepper, jalapeno, and sea salt into a Dutch oven and cook over medium-high heat until soft. Transfer the mixture into the slow cooker and ass in the remaining ingredients and cook for 2 hours on low settings.

Shred the chicken, then top with the cilantro, avocado slices and serve.

Nutrition (per Serving): Calories 240 Carbs 26g Fat 5g Protein 28g

Chicken Chile Verde

Prep Time: 12 minutes | Cooking Time: 6 hours

Ingredients (6 Servings):

- 2 lb. chopped boneless chicken
- 3 tbsp divided butter
- 3 tbsp neatly chopped & divided cilantro
- 5 minced & divided garlic cloves
- 1 extra tbsp cilantro, to garnish
- 1 ½ cups salsa Verde

Directions

Dissolve 2 tbsp butter in the slow cooker on high.

Add in 4 of the garlic along with 2 tbsp cilantro then stir.

Use a stovetop, melt 1 tbsp butter in a big frypan over medium-high heat, and add 1 tbsp minced garlic and cilantro. Put in the chopped chicken, then sear until all the sides are browned but not cooked through. Add the cilantro, garlic, and butter mixture with browned chicken into the slow cooker. Pour in the salsa Verde and stir together. Cover the slow cooker and cook on high settings for 2 hours, then reduce to a low setting for 3-4 extra hours.

Serve the chicken Verde in a lettuce cup or over cauliflower rice.

Nutrition (per Serving): Calories 305 Carbs 3g Fat 10g Protein 45g

Cauliflower & Ham Stew

Prep Time: 5 minutes | Cooking Time: 4 hours

Ingredients (6 Servings):

- 16 oz bag frozen cauliflower florets
- ¼ cup heavy cream
- ½ tsp onion powder
- ½ tsp garlic powder
- 3 cups diced ham
- 4 garlic cloves
- 8 oz grated cheddar cheese
- 14 ½ oz chicken broth
- a dash peppers

Directions:

Put all the items except the cauliflower inside the slow cooker and mix. Cover the slow cooker then cook for 4 hours on high setting. Once done, add in the cauliflower and cook for an extra 30 minutes on high. Serve and enjoy.

Nutrition (per Serving): Calories 295 Carbs 2g Fat 24g Protein 16g

Italian Minestrone Ground Beef Soup

Prep Time: 15 minutes | Cooking Time: 8 hours

Ingredients (4 Servings):

- 1 lb. ground beef
- ½ tsp basil, dried
- ½ tsp oregano, dried
- ½ cup vegetable broth
- 1 diced carrot
- 1 diced yellow onion
- 1 diced celery stalk
- 1 tbsp garlic, minced
- 1 (28 oz) can diced tomatoes
- 2 diced small zucchini

Directions:

Using a medium-sized pan on a stovetop, place in the ground beef and brown. Boil 3 cups of water. Transfer the boiled water and browned beef into the slow cooker. Put in the remaining fixing into the slow cooker. Cook for 5-8 hours on low settings. Serve and enjoy.

Nutrition (per Serving): Calories 330 Carbs 34g Fat 14g Protein 17g

Vegetable Stew

Prep Time: 15 minutes | Cooking Time: 6 hours

Ingredients (4 Servings):

- ½ cauliflower, cut into florets
- 1 red bell peppers, chopped
- 1 carrot, sliced
- 1 parsnip, cubed
- 1 tbsp olive oil
- 1 onion, chopped
- 2 garlic cloves, chopped
- ½ zucchini, cubed
- ½ cup cherry tomatoes, halved
- ¼ cup tomato sauce, no sugar added
- 1 cup vegetable stock
- 1 bay leaf
- 2 tbsp butter

Directions:

Heat-up the oil, then put the onion and garlic in a skillet. Cook for 2 minutes to soften, then place in the Slow cooker. Add the remaining ingredients, mix, and season with salt and pepper, then cook on low within 6 hours. Serve.

Nutrition (per Serving): Calories 176 Fat 5.7g Carbs 25g Protein 1.3g

Delicious Beef Meatball and Sour Cream Soup

Prep Time: 15 minutes | Cooking Time: 6 hours

Ingredients (4 Servings):

- 1 diced red bell pepper
- 8-10 halved pearl onions
- 2 cloves minced garlic
- 2 tbsp olive oil
- 3 cups lean ground beef
- 1 large egg

- 1 tsp of dry savory
- 1 cup of beef broth
- 2 cups of hot water
- 1 cup of sour cream

Directions:

Preheat the slow cooker on low. Add the oil and vegetables. Mix the egg, dry savory, and meat in a large bowl. Shape into approximately 30 small meatballs. Cook the broth in a pot, add the meatballs and cook for 2 minutes. Add the broth and the meatballs to the slow cooker then cover and cook for 6 hours. Take out a spoonful of the broth, add it to the sour cream, mix, and then put it back inside the slow cooker. Stir gently, spoon into bowls and serve.

Nutrition (per Serving): Carbs 6 g Protein 27 g Fat 32 g Calories 422

Veggie Soup with Minty Balls

Prep Time: 15 minutes | Cooking Time: 6 hours

Ingredients (4 Servings):

- 3 cups of beef broth
- 1 medium zucchini sliced into sticks
- 2 diced celery sticks
- 1 diced yellow onion
- 5 crushed cloves of garlic
- 1 cubed medium tomato
- 3 cups of ground veal
- ½ cup of Parmesan cheese
- 1 large egg
- ½ cup of chopped fresh mint
- 1 tsp of dry oregano
- 1 tsp of sweet paprika

Directions:

Preheat the slow cooker on low. Add the tomato, onion, celery, zucchini, and broth.

Mix the meat, salt, pepper, seasoning, mint, egg, garlic, and cheese in a large bowl. Shape the meat into small, approximately 40 small meatballs. Heat-up the olive oil in a pan, then put the meatballs and brown. Put the meatballs inside the slow cooker, then put one cup of hot water if more liquid is required. Cook within 6-8 hours, low. Spoon into bowls and serve.

Nutrition (per Serving): Carbs 5 g Protein 32 g Fat 25 g Calories 395 g

Chicken Cordon Bleu Soup

Prep Time: 15 minutes | Cooking Time: 6 hours

Ingredients (6 Servings):

- 12 oz diced ham
- 1 lb. chicken breast
- 4 oz diced onion
- 5 oz chopped mushrooms
- 3 tbsp minced garlic
- 6 cups chicken broth
- 2 tsp tarragon
- 3 tbsp salted butter
- 1 ½ cups heavy cream
- ½ cup sour cream
- ½ cup grated parmesan cheese
- 4 oz Swiss cheese

Directions:

Place the onion, tarragon, salt, pepper, ham, mushroom, and broth into the slow cooker. Heat-up the butter in a saucepan, then sauté the garlic. Add the chicken and sear it. Place the chicken, garlic, and cheese in the slow cooker—cover and cook on low within six hours.

Add cream and cook for another hour. Serve.

Nutrition (per Serving): Calories 518 Fat 42 g Carbs 2.75 g Protein 36 g

Ginger Pumpkin Soup

Prep Time: 15 minutes | Cooking Time: 4 hours

Ingredients (4 Servings):

- 1 lb. pumpkin chunks
- 1 diced onion
- 1 tsp crushed ginger
- 1 tsp crushed garlic
- ½ stick butter
- 2 cups vegetable stock
- 1 2/3 cups of coconut cream

Directions:

Place all the items inside a slow cooker. Cook on high for 4-6 hours. Puree the soup using an immersion blender. Spoon into bowls and serve.

Nutrition (per Serving): Calories 64 Fat 2.7 g Carbs 5.4 g Protein 2.3 g

S A L T & P E P P E R *the list of ingredient list do not indicate the amount of salt and pepper: you can add approximately a teaspoon of salt and, in if you like it, 1/2 teaspoon of pepper for each recipe*

CHAPTER 3: VEGETABLES AND SIDE DISHES

Spinach-Feta Quiche

Prep Time: 20 minutes | Cooking Time: 7 to 8 hours

Ingredients (4 Servings):

- 8 eggs
- 2 cups fresh spinach
- 2 cups of milk
- ½ cup shredded Parmesan cheese
- ¾ cup crumbled feta cheese
- ¼ cup shredded cheddar cheese
- 2 garlic cloves, minced

Directions:

Mix the eggs plus milk in a large bowl. Add the spinach, feta cheese, garlic, Parmesan cheese, and then stir until well combined. Put the batter into the greased slow cooker then sprinkle cheddar cheese on top.

Cover then cook for 7 to 8 hours on low.

Nutrition (per Serving): Calories 357 Carbs 9.4g Protein 25g Fat 22.4g

Cheesy Zucchini-Asparagus Frittata

Prep Time: 30 minutes |Cooking Time: 1 H 10 minutes

Ingredients (6 Servings):

- 8 oz asparagus, trimmed then sliced diagonally into 2" pieces
- 3 tbsp olive oil
- 1 medium-size zucchini, cut into ½" thickness
- 2 medium-size shallots, diced
- 12 large eggs
- 1 cup Parmesan cheese, grated
- ¼ cup minced fresh basil (or flat-leaf parsley leaves)

Directions:

Heat-up oil in a medium-size skillet over medium-high heat then add the asparagus, shallots, and zucchini. Cook for some minutes until the asparagus starts to soften and the zucchini a bit browned. Remove the veggies from heat then let it cool for 10 minutes. Grease the bottom and sides of your slow cooker using a cooking spray and then pour the cooled veggies into it.

Beat the eggs, basil, and parmesan together in a medium-size bowl and then put the batter inside the slow cooker. Mix until the veggies are well mixed. Cover the cooker then cook for 60 to 70 minutes on high until ready. Slice into 4 portions, then use a spatula to lift it out into plates. Serve at once.

Nutrition (per Serving): Calories 220 Carbs 4g Protein 18g Fat 17g

Slow-Cooked Yellow Squash Zucchini

Prep Time: 5 minutes | Cooking Time: 6 hours

Ingredients (4 Servings):

- 2 medium yellow squash, sliced and quartered
- 2 medium zucchinis, sliced and quartered
- ¼ tsp pepper
- 1 tsp Italian seasoning
- 1 tsp powdered garlic
- ¼ cup Parmesan cheese, grated
- ¼ cup butter, cubed

Directions:

Combine the sliced yellow squash and zucchini in your slow cooker. Sprinkle Italian seasoning, and garlic powder on top.

Place the butter pieces, and cheese on top. Cover the cooker then cook for 4 to 6 hours on low.

Nutrition (per Serving): Calories 45 Carbs 5.4g Protein 4.2g Fat 2.9g

Cabbage, Kielbasa, and Onion Soup

Prep Time: 5 minutes | Cooking Time: 8 hours

Ingredients (6 Servings):

- 2 ½ lb. cabbage head, cut into wedges
- 1 cup vegetable broth
- 1 onion, thinly sliced
- 1 tbsp brown mustard
- ½ tsp black pepper
- 1 lb. kielbasa (or any sausages) sliced into 3-inch pieces
- Cooking spray, as required

Directions:

Put all the items in the slow cooker, excluding the kielbasa, and combine them well.

Make sure that the cabbage is well coated with the seasoning broth mixture. Now, top it with the kielbasa and cover the slow cooker. Cook for 7 hours on low heat. Stir it again and cook it for an additional 1 hour.

Nutrition (per Serving): Calories 278 Carbs 11g Protein 16.8g Fat 15g

Parmesan Mushrooms

Prep Time: 5 minutes | Cooking Time: 4 hours

Ingredients (4 Servings):

- 16 oz cremini mushrooms, fresh
- ½ oz ranch dressing mix
- 2 tbsp parmesan cheese, add more if desired
- ½ cup butter, melted and unsalted

Directions:

Place the mushrooms in the slow cooker. Combine melted butter and ranch dressing in a small-sized bowl. Stir in the butter mixture over the mushrooms and mix well.

Now, toss the parmesan cheese over the top. Cover the slow cooker and cook for 4 hours on low heat.

Nutrition (per Serving): Calories 240 Carbs 4g Protein 4.9g Fat 24g

Mashed Garlic Cauliflower

Prep Time: 5 minutes | Cooking Time: 6 hours

Ingredients (6 Servings):

- 2 medium cauliflower head, sliced into florets
- 3 tbsp butter
- 4 garlic cloves
- 8 to 10 cups of water
- Dill, to taste

Directions:

Place the garlic and cauliflower along with a sufficient amount of water in the slow cooker.

Cook within 6 hours on low heat or until the cauliflower becomes tender.

Discard the water then place the cauliflower in the food processor. Add butter, then pulse until it is mashed. Now, to this, stir in the seasoning and check for taste. Finally, toss the herbs into it and serve it immediately.

Nutrition (per Serving): Calories 28 Carbs 0.5g Protein 0.2g Fat 1.4g

Zucchini Pasta

Prep Time: 15 minutes | Cooking Time: 2 hours

Ingredients (4 Servings):

- 2 lb. spiralized zucchini
- ¼ cup olive oil
- ½ cup basil
- ½ tsp red pepper flakes
- 1-pint halved cherry tomatoes
- 1 sliced red onion
- 4 minced garlic cloves

Directions:

Sauté onion and garlic 3 minutes in olive oil.

Add zucchini noodles to your slow cooker and season with pepper and salt—Cook 60 minutes on high heat. Mix in tomatoes, basil, onion, garlic, and red pepper. Cook another 20 minutes. Add parmesan cheese to slow cooker. Mix thoroughly and cook 10 minutes to melt the cheese. Serve.

Nutrition (per Serving): Calories 111 Carbs 6g Fat 13g Protein 5g

Twice Baked Spaghetti Squash

Prep Time: 15 minutes | Cooking Time: 6 hours

Ingredients (4 Servings):

- ½ cup grated parmesan cheese
- 2 small spaghetti squashes
- 1 tsp oregano

- 2 minced garlic cloves
- 2 tbsp butter
- 4 slices Provolone cheese

Directions:

Cut spaghetti squash in half lengthwise, discarding innards. Set gently into your pot.

Cook on high heat for 4 hours. Take squash innards and mix with parmesan cheese and butter. Then mix in pepper, salt, garlic, and oregano. Add squash innards mixture to the middle of cooked squash halves. Cook on high for another 1-2 hours till middles are deliciously bubbly.

Nutrition (per Serving): Calories 155 Carbs 4g Fat 12g Protein 12g

Mushroom Risotto

Prep Time: 15 minutes | Cooking Time: 3 hours

Ingredients (4 Servings):

- ¼ cup vegetable broth
- 1lb. sliced Portobello mushrooms
- 1lb. sliced white mushrooms
- 1/3 cup grated parmesan cheese
- 2 diced shallots
- 3 tbsp chopped chives
- 3 tbsp coconut oil
- 4 ½ cup riced cauliflower
- 4 tbsp butter

Directions:

Heat-up oil and sauté mushrooms 3 minutes till soft. Discard liquid and set it to the side.

Add oil to skillet and sauté shallots 60 seconds. Pour all recipe components into your pot and mix well to combine. Cook 3 hours on high heat. Serve topped with parmesan cheese.

Nutrition (per Serving): Calories 185 Carbs 5g Fat 14g Protein 5g

Veggie Bowl

Prep Time: 15 minutes | Cooking Time: 45 minutes

Ingredients (4 Servings):

- ½ cucumber, sliced into strips
- 1 grated carrot
- 1 sliced red bell pepper
- 1 tbsp soy sauce
- 1 tsp sesame oil
- 10 oz riced cauliflower
- 2 tbsp rice vinegar
- 2 tbsp sesame seeds
- 2 tbsp sriracha sauce
- 4-5 broccoli florets
- 7 oz tempeh, sliced into squares
- liquid sweetener

Directions:

In a bowl, combine tempeh squares with 1 tbsp soy sauce and 2 tbsp vinegar. Set aside to soak. Slice veggies.

Add carrot, broccoli, and peppers to slow cooker. Cook on high 30 minutes. Add cauliflower rice to the slow cooker; cook 5 minutes. Add sweetener, oil, soy sauce, vinegar, and sriracha to slow cooker. Don't hesitate to add a bit of water if you find the mixture to be too thick.

Nutrition (per Serving): Calories 119 Carbs 40g Fat 38g Protein 68g

Avocado Pesto Noodles

Prep Time: 15 minutes | Cooking Time: 1 hour

Ingredients (2 Servings):

- ¼ cup basil
- ½ cup extra-virgin olive oil
- 1 avocado
- 1 cup baby spinach leaves
- 1-2 garlic cloves

- 1 package of kelp noodles

Directions:

Add kelp noodles to slow cooker with just enough water to cover them. Cook on high 45-60 minutes. In the meantime, combine pesto ingredients in a blender, blending till smooth and incorporated. Stir in pesto and heat noodle mixture 10 minutes.

Nutrition (per Serving): Calories 315 Carbs 7g Fat 32g Protein 2g

Vegan Cream of Mushroom Soup

Prep Time: 15 minutes | Cooking Time: 1 hour

Ingredients (2 Servings):

- ½ diced yellow onion
- ½ tsp extra-virgin olive oil
- 1 ½ cup chopped white mushrooms
- 1 2/3 cup unsweetened almond milk
- 1 tsp onion powder
- 2 cup cauliflower florets

Directions:

Add cauliflower, onion powder, and milk to slow cooker. Stir and set to cook on high 1 hour. With olive oil, sauté onions and mushrooms together 8 to 10 minutes till softened. Allow cauliflower mixture to cool off a bit and add to blender. Blend until smooth. Then blend in mushroom mixture. Pour back into the slow cooker and heat 30 minutes.

Nutrition (per Serving): Calories 110 Carbs 9g Fat 8g Protein 3g

Creamy Curry Noodle Bowl

Prep Time: 15 minutes | Cooking Time: 2 hours

Ingredients (4 Servings):

- ½ head chopped cauliflower

- 1 diced red bell pepper
- 1 pack Noodles
- 3 chopped carrots
- 2 handfuls of mixed greens

Curry Sauce:

- ¼ cup mayo
- ¼ cup water
- ¼ tsp ginger
- 1 tsp coriander
- 1 tsp cumin
- 1 tsp turmeric
- 2 tbsp apple cider vinegar
- 2 tbsp avocado oil
- 2 tsp curry powder

Directions:

Add all ingredients, minus curry sauce components, to your slow cooker. Set to cook on high 1-2 hours. In the meantime, add all the curry sauce ingredients to a blender. Puree until smooth. Pour over veggie and noodle mixture. Stir well to coat.

Nutrition (per Serving): Calories 110 Carbs 13g Fat 6g Protein 2g

Spinach and Artichoke Casserole

Prep Time: 15 minutes | Cooking Time: 4 hours

Ingredients (10 Servings):

- ¾ cup coconut flour
- ¾ cup unsweetened almond milk
- 1 cup grated parmesan cheese
- 1 tbsp baking powder
- 3 minced garlic cloves
- 5 oz chopped spinach
- 6 oz chopped artichoke hearts
- 6 eggs

Directions:

Grease the inside of your slow cooker.

Whisk ½ of parmesan cheese, garlic, artichoke hearts, spinach, eggs, and almond milk. Add baking powder and coconut flour, combining well. Spread into the slow cooker. Sprinkle with remaining parmesan cheese. Cook within 2 to 3 hours on high, or you can cook 4 to 6 hours on a lower heat setting.

Nutrition (per Serving): Calories 141 Carbs 7g Fat 9g Protein 9g

Lemony Asparagus

Prep Time: 15 minutes | Cooking Time: 2 hours

Ingredients (2 Servings):

- 1 lb. asparagus spears
- 1 tbsp lemon juice

Directions:

Prepare the seasonings and crush 2 cloves of garlic and salt and pepper to taste.

Put the asparagus spears on the bottom of the slow cooker. Add the lemon juice and the seasonings. Cook on low for 2 hours.

Nutrition (per Serving): Calories 48 Fat 2 g Carbs 8.7 g Protein 4.5 g

Veggie-Noodle Soup

Prep Time: 15 minutes | Cooking Time: 8 hours

Ingredients (2 Servings):

- ½ cup chopped carrots, chopped
- ½ cup chopped celery, chopped
- 1 tsp Italian seasoning
- 7 oz zucchini, cut spiral
- 2 cups spinach leaves, chopped

Directions:

Except for the zucchini and spinach, add all the ingredients to the slow cooker.

Add 3 cups of water. Cover and cook within 8 hours on low. Add the zucchini and spinach at the last 10 minutes of cooking.

Nutrition (per Serving): Calories 56 Fat 0.5 g Carbs 1g Protein 3 g

Zucchini and Yellow Squash

Prep Time: 15 minutes | Cooking Time: 6 hours

Ingredients (2 Servings):

- 2/3 cup zucchini, sliced
- 2/3 cups yellow squash, sliced
- 1/3 tsp Italian seasoning
- 1/8 cup butter

Directions:

Place zucchini and squash on the bottom of the slow cooker. Sprinkle with the Italian seasoning with salt, pepper, and garlic powder to taste. Top with butter. Cover and cook within 6 hours on low.

Nutrition (per Serving): Calories 122 Fat 9.9 g Carbs 3.7 g Protein 4.2 g

Gluten-Free Zucchini Bread

Prep Time: 15 minutes | Cooking Time: 3 hours

Ingredients (2 Servings):

- ½ cup coconut flour
- ½ tsp baking powder and baking soda
- 1 egg, whisked
- ¼ cup butter
- 1 cup zucchini, shredded

Directions:

Combine all dry ingredients and add a pinch of salt. Combine them with the eggs and mix thoroughly.

Fold in zucchini and spread inside the slow cooker. Cover and cook within 3 hours on high.

Nutrition (per Serving): Calories 400 Fat 30 g Carbs 23.9 g Protein 10 g

Eggplant Parmesan

Prep Time: 40 minutes | Cooking Time: 4 hours

Ingredients (2 Servings):

- 1 large eggplant, 1/2-inch slices
- 1 egg, whisked
- 1 tsp Italian seasoning
- 1 cup marinara
- ¼ cup Parmesan cheese, grated

Directions:

Put salt on each side of the eggplant, then let stand for 30 minutes.

Spread some of the marinara on the bottom of the slow cooker and season with garlic powder, and Italian seasoning. Spread the eggplants on a single the slow cooker and pour over some of the marinara sauce. Repeat up to 3 layers. Top with Parmesan. Cover and cook for 4 hours.

Nutrition (per Serving): Calories 159 Fat 12 g Carbs 13 g Protein 14 g

Zucchini Lasagna

Prep Time: 15 minutes | Cooking Time: 4 hours

Ingredients (2 Servings):

- 1 large egg, whisked
- 1/8 cup Parmesan cheese, grated
- 1 cup spinach, chopped
- 2 cups tomato sauce

- 2 zucchinis, 1/8-inch thick, pre-grilled

Directions:

Mix egg with spinach and parmesan. Spread some of the tomato sauce inside the slow cooker and season with salt and pepper. Spread the zucchini on a single the slow cooker and pour over some of the tomato sauce. Repeat until 3 layers. Top with Parmesan. Cover and cook for 4 hours.

Nutrition (per Serving): Calories 351 Fat 4.9 g Carbs 64.8 g Protein 8.8 g

Cauliflower Bolognese on Zucchini Noodles

Prep Time: 15 minutes | Cooking Time: 4 hours

Ingredients (3 Servings):

- 1 cauliflower head, floret cuts
- 1 tsp dried basil flakes
- 28 oz diced tomatoes
- ½ cup vegetable broth
- 5 zucchinis, spiral cut
- 2 garlic cloves

Directions:

Place the ingredients in the slow cooker except for the zucchini. Season with 2 garlic cloves, salt, pepper to taste, and desired spices. Cover and cook for 4 hours. Smash florets of the cauliflower with a fork to form "Bolognese." Transfer the dish on top of the zucchini noodles.

Nutrition (per Serving): Calories 405 Fat 5 g Carbs 76 g Protein 12 g

Tomato, Zucchini, and Yellow Squash

Prep Time: 15 minutes | Cooking Time: 6 hours

Ingredients (3 Servings):

- 1 medium yellow squash, quartered, sliced
- 1 medium zucchini, quartered, sliced
- 1 tomato, cut into wedges
- ½ tsp Italian seasoning
- 2 tbsp parmesan cheese, grated
- ½ tsp garlic powder
- 2 tbsp cold butter, cubed

Directions:

Add squash, tomato, and zucchini in the slow cooker. Sprinkle salt, garlic powder, and Italian seasoning. Place butter cubes all over the vegetables, then sprinkle cheese on top. Close the lid. Cook on 'Low' for 4-6 hours or until tender. Stir and serve.

Nutrition (per Serving): Calories126 Fat 10.2g Carbs 6g Protein 4.9g

Parmesan Zucchini Gratin

Prep Time: 15 minutes | Cooking Time: 4 hours

Ingredients (3 Servings):

- 3 small zucchinis, sliced
- 1 small onion, chopped
- 1 medium tomato, sliced
- ¼ cup parmesan cheese, shredded
- 1 tbsp garlic, minced
- ½ tsp garlic powder
- 1 tsp dried basil
- 1 tbsp olive oil + extra to drizzle

Directions:

Place a skillet over medium heat. Put the oil, then onions, and cook until soft. Add garlic and cook until fragrant. Transfer into the slow cooker. Place alternate layers of zucchini slices and a tomato slice. Drizzle olive oil all over the top layer. Sprinkle dried herbs, garlic powder, and finally, Parmesan cheese. Close the lid. Cook on 'Low' for 3-4 hours or until tender.

Nutrition (per Serving): Calories 89 Fat 5.5g Carbs 9.1g Protein 3.1g

Slow-Cooked Vegetables

Prep Time: 15 minutes | Cooking Time: 45 minutes

Ingredients (5 Servings):

- 1 cup okra slices
- 1 medium onion, chopped into chunks
- 1 medium zucchini, sliced
- ½ cup grape tomatoes
- 1 yellow bell pepper, sliced
- ½ cup mushroom, sliced
- ¼ cup olive oil
- ¼ cup balsamic vinegar
- ½ tbsp fresh thyme, chopped
- 1 tbsp fresh basil, chopped

Directions:

Put all the fixings into the slow cooker and stir well. Close the lid. Cook on 'High' for 45 minutes. Serve.

Nutrition (per Serving): Calories 125 Fat 10.4g Carbs 7.9g Protein 1.8g

Cheesy Cauliflower Bread

Prep Time: 15 minutes | Cooking Time: 4 hours

Ingredients (6 Servings):

- 1 ½ lb. cauliflower, grated to a rice-like texture
- 4 cups mozzarella cheese, shredded, divided
- 2 tsp garlic
- 2 tsp red pepper flakes
- 6 tsp Italian seasoning
- 6 tbsp coconut flour
- 4 large eggs, beaten

- Cooking spray

Directions:

Grease the instant pot with cooking spray. Add all the ingredients (left out 2 cups of cheese and garlic) into a bowl and mix it until well. Transfer into the slow cooker. Scatter garlic and remaining cheese on top. Close the lid. Cook on 'High' for 2-4 hours or until brown and crisp. Cut slices and serve.

Nutrition (per Serving): Calories 314 Fat 19g Carbs 9.5g Protein 23.7g

Cheesy Cauliflower Gratin

Prep Time: 15 minutes | Cooking Time: 4 hours

Ingredients (4 Servings):

- 2 cups cauliflower florets
- 3 tbsp heavy whipping cream
- 4 slices pepper Jack cheese
- 2 tbsp butter

Directions:

Add cauliflower, cream, butter into the slow cooker. Close the lid. Cook on 'Low' for 3-4 hours or until tender. When done, mash with a fork. Taste and adjust the seasoning if necessary. Place cheese slices on top. Cover and cook within 10 minutes or until cheese melts. Serve right away.

Nutrition (per Serving): Calories 132 Fat 19.3g Carbs 4g Protein 5.7g

Creamy Spaghetti Squash

Prep Time: 15 minutes | Cooking Time: 6 hours

Ingredients (4 Servings):

- 2 spaghetti squash, halved, deseeded
- 2 tsp garlic powder

- 3 tbsp fresh basil or parsley, chopped
- 2 cups ricotta cheese
- 2 tsp lemon zest, grated
- Cooking spray

Directions:

Spray the cut part of the spaghetti squash with cooking spray. Place it in the slow cooker with the cut side facing down. Close the lid. Cook on 'Low' for 4-6 hours or until tender. When done, using a fork, scrape the squash, and add into a bowl.

Add ricotta cheese, lemon zest, garlic powder, salt, pepper, and basil and mix well.

Nutrition (per Serving): Calories 112 Fat 5.4g Carbs 2.1g Protein 7.7g

Creamy Keto Cauliflower

Prep Time: 15 minutes | Cooking Time: 2 hours

Ingredients (8 Servings):

- 2 large heads cauliflower, chopped into small floret's
- 3 cloves garlic, minced
- 1 large onion, chopped
- 6 tbsp butter or ghee+ extra to top
- 1 cup cream cheese or sour cream
- ½ cup of water

Directions:

Place the cauliflower florets in the slow cooker. Pour about ½ a cup of water.

Close the lid. Cook on 'Low' for 1-2 hours or until tender. Place a skillet over medium heat. Add 2 tbsp butter or ghee. When it melts, add onions and garlic and sauté until the onions are translucent. Add remaining butter and stir, then remove from heat. Transfer into a blender. Add cauliflower and blend until smooth or blend in the food processor. Add cream cheese and pulse until well combined. Transfer into a bowl, then add salt and pepper to taste. Top with butter plus ghee and serve.

Nutrition (per Serving): Calories 199 Fat 21.7g Carbs 4.3g Protein 3.1g

Ranch Mushrooms

Prep Time: 15 minutes | Cooking Time: 2 hours

Ingredients (2 Servings):

- 1 package of Ranch Dressing
- 4 packages of whole mushrooms
- 1 cube butter, melted

Directions:

Place 5 cloves of garlic at the bottom of the slow cooker and pour in the melted butter.

Add in the mushrooms and pour the dressing—season with salt and pepper to taste.

Cover and cook on high within 2 hours.

Nutrition (per Serving): Calories 97 Fat 20 g Carbs 3 g Protein 10 g

Creamed Spinach

Prep Time: 15 minutes | Cooking Time: 3 hours

Ingredients (3 Servings):

- 8 oz spinach, defrosted
- 3 tbsp Parmesan cheese
- 3 oz cream cheese
- 2 tbsp sour cream

Directions:

Combine all the fixings in the slow cooker. Add some seasonings: half a tsp of onion and garlic powder. Mix thoroughly—cover and cook within 3 hours on low.

Nutrition (per Serving): Calories 282 Fat 27.22 g Carbs 3.63 g Protein 7.33 g

Zoodles with Cauliflower Sauce

Prep Time: 15 minutes | Cooking Time: 3 hours

Ingredients (4 Servings):

- 5 large spiralized zucchinis
- 2 24-oz cans of diced tomatoes
- 2 small heads cauliflower florets
- 1 cup chopped sweet onion
- 2 minced garlic cloves
- ½ cup veggie broth
- 6 tsp Italian seasoning
- Enough water to cover zoodles

Directions:

Put everything but the zoodles into your slow cooker. Cook on high for 3 ½ hours. Smash into a chunky sauce with a potato masher or another utensil. To cook the zoodles, boil a large pot of water. When boiling, cook zoodles for just 1 minute, then drain—Season with salt and pepper. Serve sauce over zoodles!

Nutrition (per Serving): Calories 313 Protein 7g Carbs 62g Fat 2g

Spaghetti Squash Carbonara

Prep Time: 15 minutes | Cooking Time: 8 hours

Ingredients (4 Servings):

- 2 cups of water
- One 3-lb. spaghetti squash
- ½ cup bacon
- ½ cup fresh spinach leaves
- 2 eggs
- 4 tbsp heavy cream

- 3 tbsp unsweetened almond milk
- ½ cup grated Parmesan cheese
- 1 tsp garlic powder

Directions:

Put squash in your cooker and pour in 2 cups of water. Close the lid. Cook on low for 8-9 hours.

When the spaghetti squash cools, mix egg, cream, milk, and cheese in a bowl. When the squash is cool enough for you to handle with oven mitts, cut it open lengthwise and scrape out noodles. Mix in the egg mixture right away. Add spinach and seasonings. Top with coconut bacon and serve!

Nutrition (per Serving): Calories 244 Protein 18g Carbs 2g Fat 17g

Bell Pepper and Eggplant Salad

Prep Time: 15 minutes | Cooking Time: 7 hours

Ingredients (4 Servings):

- 1 14-oz can of whole tomatoes
- 2 sliced yellow bell peppers
- 3 small eggplants
- 1 sliced red onion
- 1 tbsp paprika
- 2 tsp cumin
- A squeeze of lime juice

Directions:

Mix all the fixings in your slow cooker. Close the lid. Cook on low for 7-8 hours. When time is up, serve warm, or chill in the fridge for a few hours before eating.

Nutrition (per Serving): Calories 188 Protein 5g Carbs 37g Fat 1g

Zucchini Pasta

Prep Time: 15 minutes | Cooking Time: 1 hour

Ingredients (2 Servings):

- 2 zucchinis
- 1 tsp dried oregano
- 1 tsp dried basil
- 2 tbsp butter
- tbsp water

Directions:

Peel the zucchini and spiralize it with a veggie spiralizer. Melt the butter and mix it together with the dried oregano, dried basil, salt, and water. Place the spiralized zucchini in the slow cooker and add the spice mixture. Close the lid and cook the meal for 1 hour on low. Let the cooked pasta cool slightly. Serve it!

Nutrition (per Serving): Calories 18 Fat 6g Carbs 3.5g Protein 1.3g

Chinese Broccoli

Prep Time: 15 minutes | Cooking Time: 1 hour

Ingredients (2 Servings):

- 1 tbsp sesame seeds
- 1 tbsp olive oil
- 2 cup broccoli
- 1 tsp chili flakes
- 1 tbsp apple cider vinegar
- 3 tbsp water
- ¼ tsp garlic powder

Directions:

Cut the broccoli into the florets and sprinkle with the olive oil, chili flakes, apple cider vinegar, and garlic powder. Stir the broccoli and place it in the slow cooker. Add water and sesame seeds. Cook the broccoli for 1 hour on high. Transfer the cooked broccoli to serving plates and enjoy!

Nutrition (per Serving): Calories 39 Fat 4.9g Carbs 5.4g Protein 2.4g

Slow cooker Spaghetti

Prep Time: 15 minutes | Cooking Time: 4 hours

Ingredients (5 Servings):

- 1 lb. spaghetti squash
- 1 tbsp butter
- ¼ cup water
- 1 tsp ground black pepper
- ¼ tsp ground nutmeg

Directions:

Peel the spaghetti squash and sprinkle it with the ground black pepper and ground nutmeg.

Pour water in the slow cooker. Add butter and spaghetti squash. Close the lid and cook for 4 hours on Low. Chop the spaghetti squash into small pieces and serve!

Nutrition (per Serving): Calories 50 Fat 2.9g Fiber 6.6g Carbs 0.1g Protein 0.7g

Mushroom Stew

Prep Time: 15 minutes | Cooking Time: 6 hours

Ingredients (8 Servings):

- 1 cup white mushrooms, sliced
- 2 eggplants, chopped
- 1 onion, diced
- 1 garlic clove, diced
- 2 bell peppers, chopped
- 1 cup water
- 1 tbsp butter

Directions:

Place the sliced mushrooms, chopped eggplant, and diced onion into the slow cooker. Add garlic clove and bell peppers. Add butter and water and stir it gently with a wooden spatula. Close the lid and cook the stew for 6 hours on low. Stir the cooked stew one more time and serve.

Nutrition (per Serving): Calories 71 Fat 1.9g Fiber 5.9g Carbs 13g Protein 3g

Cabbage Steaks

Prep Time: 15 minutes | Cooking Time: 2 hours

Ingredients (4 Servings):

- 1 white cabbage
- 1 tbsp butter
- ½ tsp cayenne pepper
- ½ tsp chili flakes
- tbsp water

Directions:

Slice the cabbage into medium steaks and rub them with the cayenne pepper and chili flakes.

Rub the cabbage steaks with butter on each side. Place them in the slow cooker and sprinkle with water. Close the lid and cook the cabbage steaks for 2 hours on high. When the cabbage steaks are cooked, they should be tender to the touch. Serve the cabbage steak after 10 minutes of chilling.

Nutrition (per Serving): Calories 44 Fat 3g Fiber 1.8g Carbs 4.3g Protein 1g

Mashed Cauliflower

Prep Time: 20 minutes | Cooking Time: 3 hours

Ingredients (5 Servings):

- 1 tbsp butter
- 1lb. cauliflower
- 1 tbsp full-fat cream

- 1 oz dill, chopped

Directions:

Wash the cauliflower and chop it. Place the chopped cauliflower in the slow cooker.

Add butter and full-fat cream. Stir the mixture and close the lid. Cook the cauliflower for 3 hours on high. When the cauliflower is cooked, transfer it to a blender and blend until smooth. Place the smooth cauliflower in a bowl and mix with the chopped dill. Stir it well and serve!

Nutrition (per Serving): Calories 101 Fat 7.4g Fiber 3.2g Carbs 8.3g Protein 3.1g

Bacon Wrapped Cauliflower

Prep Time: 15 minutes | Cooking Time: 7 hours

Ingredients (4 Servings):

- 1 cauliflower head
- 10 slices bacon
- 1 tsp salt
- 1 tsp cayenne pepper
- 1 tbsp butter, softened
- ¾ cup water

Directions:

Sprinkle the cauliflower head with the salt and cayenne pepper then rub with butter. Wrap the cauliflower head in the sliced bacon and secure with toothpicks. Pour water in the slow cooker and add the wrapped cauliflower head. Cook the cauliflower head for 7 hours on low.

Then let the cooked cauliflower head cool for 10 minutes. Serve it!

Nutrition (per Serving): Calories 187 Fat 14.8g Fiber 2.1g Carbs 4.7g Protein 9.5g

Cauliflower Casserole

Prep Time: 15 minutes | Cooking Time: 7 hours

Ingredients (5 Servings):

- 2 tomatoes, chopped
- 1 cauliflower chopped
- 1 cup broccoli, chopped
- 1 cup water
- 1 tbsp butter
- 1 cup white mushrooms, chopped
- 1 tsp chili flakes

Directions:

Mix the water, salt, and chili flakes. Place the butter in the slow cooker. Add a layer of the chopped cauliflower. Add the layer of broccoli and tomatoes. Add the mushrooms and pat down the mix to flatten. Add the water and close the lid. Cook the casserole for 7 hours on low. Cool the casserole to room temperature and serve!

Nutrition (per Serving): Calories 61 Fat 2.6g Fiber 3.2g Carbs 8.1g Protein 3.4g

Cauliflower Rice

Prep Time: 15 minutes | Cooking Time: 2 hours

Ingredients (5 Servings):

- 1lb. cauliflower
- 1 tbsp turmeric
- 1 tbsp butter
- ¾ cup water

Directions:

Chop the cauliflower into tiny pieces to make cauliflower rice. You can also pulse in a food processor to get very fine grains of 'rice'. Place the cauliflower rice in the slow cooker.

Add salt, turmeric, and water. Stir gently and close the lid. Cook the cauliflower rice for 2 hours on high. Strain the cauliflower rice and transfer it to a bowl. Add butter and stir gently. Serve it!

Nutrition (per Serving): Calories 48 Fat 2.5g Fiber 2.6g Carbs 5.7g Protein 1.9g

Curry Cauliflower

Prep Time: 15 minutes | Cooking Time: 5 hours

Ingredients (2 Servings):

- 1 cauliflower
- 1 tsp curry paste
- 1 tsp curry powder
- ½ tsp dried cilantro
- 1 oz butter
- ¾ cup water
- ¼ cup chicken stock

Directions:

Chop the cauliflower roughly and sprinkle it with the curry powder and dried cilantro.

Place the chopped cauliflower in the slow cooker. Mix the curry paste with the water.

Add chicken stock and transfer the liquid to the slow cooker. Add butter and close the lid.

Cook the cauliflower for 5 hours on Low. Strain ½ of the liquid off and discard. Transfer the cauliflower to serving bowls. Serve it!

Nutrition (per Serving): Calories 158 Fat 13.3g Fiber 3.9g Carbs 8.9g Protein 3.3g

Garlic Cauliflower Steaks

Prep Time: 15 minutes | Cooking Time: 3 hours

Ingredients (4 Servings):

- 1 cauliflower head
- 1 tsp minced garlic
- 1 tbsp butter
- 3 tbsp water
- 1 tsp paprika

Directions:

Wash the cauliflower head carefully and slice it into the medium steaks. Mix up together the butter, minced garlic, and paprika. Rub the cauliflower steaks with the butter mixture.

Pour the water in the slow cooker. Add the cauliflower steaks and close the lid. Cook the vegetables for 3 hours on High. Transfer the cooked cauliflower steaks to a platter and serve them immediately!

Nutrition (per Serving): Calories 129 Fat 11.7g Fiber 2.7g Carbs 5.8g Protein 2.2g

Zucchini Gratin

Prep Time: 10 minutes | Cooking Time: 5 hours

Ingredients (3 Servings):

- 1 zucchini, sliced
- Parmesan, grated
- 1 tbsp butter
- ½ cup almond milk

Directions:

Sprinkle the sliced zucchini with the ground black pepper. Chop the butter and place it in the slow cooker. Transfer the sliced zucchini to the slow cooker to make the bottom layer.

Add the almond milk. Sprinkle the zucchini with the grated cheese and close the lid.

Cook the gratin for 5 hours on Low. Then let the gratin cool until room temperature. Serve it!

Nutrition (per Serving): Calories 229 Fat 19.6g Fiber 1.8g Carbs 5.9g Protein 10.9g

Eggplant Gratin

Prep Time: 15 minutes | Cooking Time: 5 hours

Ingredients (4 Servings):

- 1 tbsp butter
- 1 tsp minced garlic
- 2 eggplants, chopped
- 1 tbsp dried parsley
- 4 tbsp Parmesan, grated
- 3tbsp water
- 1 tsp chili flakes

Directions:

Mix the dried parsley, chili flakes, and salt together.

Sprinkle the chopped eggplants with the spice mixture and stir well. Place the eggplants in the slow cooker. Add the water and minced garlic. Add the butter and sprinkle with the grated Parmesan. Close the lid and cook the gratin for 5 hours on Low. Open it and cool the gratin for 10 minutes. Serve it.

Nutrition (per Serving): Calories 107 Fat 5.4g Fiber 5.6g Carbs 10g Protein 6.8g

Moroccan Eggplant

Prep Time: 15 minutes | Cooking Time: 7 hours

Ingredients (4 Servings):

- 2 eggplants, peeled
- 1 jalapeno pepper
- 1 tsp curry powder
- 1 tsp paprika
- ¾ tsp ground nutmeg
- 2 tbsp butter
- ¾ cup almond milk
- 1 tsp dried dill

Directions:

Chop the eggplant into small pieces. Place the eggplant in the slow cooker. Chop the jalapeno pepper and combine it with the eggplant. Then sprinkle the vegetables with the curry powder, paprika, ground nutmeg, and dried dill. Add almond milk and butter.

Close the lid and cook the vegetables for 7 hours on Low. Cool the vegetables and then blend them until smooth with a hand blender. Transfer the cooked eggplant mash into the bowls and serve!

Nutrition (per Serving): Calories 190 Fat 17g Fiber 5.6g Carbs 10g Protein 2.5g

Sautée Bell Peppers

Prep Time: 15 minutes | Cooking Time: 5 hours

Ingredients (6 Servings):

- 4 bell peppers
- 1 cauliflower, chopped
- 2 oz bacon, chopped
- ¾ cup coconut milk, unsweetened
- 1 tsp butter
- 1 tsp thyme
- 1 onion, diced
- 1 tsp turmeric

Directions:

Remove the seeds from the bell peppers and chop them roughly.

Place the bell peppers, cauliflower, and bacon in the slow cooker. Add coconut milk, butter, milk, and thyme.

Stir well then add the diced onion. Add the turmeric and stir the mixture. Close the lid and cook 5 hours on Low. When the meal is cooked, let it chill for 10 minutes and serve it!

Nutrition (per Serving): Calories 113 Fat 7.2g Carbs 10.1g Protein 5.7g

Garlic Artichoke

Prep Time: 15 minutes | Cooking Time: 2 hours

Ingredients (4 Servings):

- 4 artichokes, trimmed, chopped
- 2 tsp butter
- 1 garlic clove, peeled
- ¼ cup water

Directions:

Chop the garlic clove. Melt the butter and mix it with the chopped garlic. Place the artichoke in the slow cooker and cover it with the butter mixture. Add water and close the lid. Cook the artichoke for 2 hours on High.

Transfer the cooked artichoke to a platter and serve!

Nutrition (per Serving): Calories 45 Fat 2g Carbs 6.4g Protein 2g

S A L T & P E P P E R *the list of ingredient list do not indicate the amount of salt and pepper: you can add approximately a teaspoon of salt and, in if you like it, 1/2 teaspoon of pepper for each recipe*

CHAPTER 4: FISH AND SHELLFISH

Garlic Tilapia

Prep Time: **15 minutes** | Cooking Time: **2 hours**

Ingredients (4 Servings):

- 4 tilapia fillets

For the garlic-butter:

- 8 tbsp butter
- 8 chopped garlic cloves
- 8 tsp chopped parsley

Directions:

Mix all the garlic-butter ingredients in a bowl.

Place each tilapia fillet in the middle of a large sheet of aluminum foil. Generously season fillets with salt and pepper. Divide the garlic butter into each fillet, then seal all the fish's sides using a foil. Place into the slow cooker. Cover with lid—Cook for 2 hours on high.

Nutrition (per Serving): Calories 309 Fat 24.1 g Protein 21.9 g Carbs 2.5 g

Tuna and Olive Tapenade

Prep Time: 15 minutes | Cooking Time: 1 hour

Ingredients (4 Servings):

- 10 oz tuna
- 5 oz pitted brine-cured black olives
- 5 oz pitted mild green olives
- 5 tbsp olive oil, and extra for the spinach
- 5 oz fresh baby spinach
- 3 fresh bay leaves
- 2 thinly sliced garlic cloves
- ¼ cup fish stock or vegetable broth
- ¼ cup dry white or rose wine
- ½ medium finely chopped onion
- 1 tsp red or white wine vinegar
- 1 orange zest

Directions:

In the slow cooker, combine the broth, wine, the 4 tbsp olive oil, bay leaves, and season. Stir to combine. Cover the slow cooker with lid and cook for 30 minutes on low. Add in the tuna. Turn to coat each piece evenly with the cooked broth wine mix. Cover and cook for 25-35 minutes on low or until the fish is opaque. Once done remove with a slotted spoon and transfer to a serving platter. Shred the fish into large flakes. Cover with foil to keep warm. Discard the cooking liquid. While the fish is cooking, put the orange zest, garlic, olives, vinegar, and the remaining 1 tbsp olive oil in a food processor. Pulse until the mix is a thick puree. When ready to serve, put the spinach in a mixing bowl. Toss with a little olive oil—season with salt and pepper. Divide into the number of servings indicated, creating a bed for the tuna. Evenly distribute the tuna flakes into the number of servings. Top with the tapenade. Serve at room temperature.

Nutrition (per Serving): Calories 414 Fat 31g Protein 25.1g Carbs 9g

Tuna Stuffed Mushroom

Prep Time: 15 minutes | Cooking Time: 5 hours

Ingredients (15 Servings):

- 8 oz shredded Italian cheese blend
- 3 tbsp mayonnaise
- 2 sliced scallions
- 3 oz softened cream cheese
- 2 lb. cleaned mushrooms
- ¼ cup minced fresh parsley
- 6 oz drained tuna
- 10 oz drained chopped artichoke hearts
- ¼ tsp hot sauce

Directions:

Place artichoke hearts, scallions, and the tuna in a mixing bowl and heat until well combined.

Then add in the Italian cheese, cream cheese, hot sauce, mayo, and parsley. Mash all your ingredients until well blended. Stuff the tuna-artichoke mix into the mushroom caps.

Place a basket-type steamer in the slow cooker. Arrange a layer of the stuffed mushrooms on the basket steamer. Take a piece of aluminum foil, then make holes in the foil using a fork. Fit the holed aluminum foil down the first layer of the stuffed mushrooms. Make a hole in the middle. Arrange another layer of stuffed mushrooms on the foil. Do the process again to ensure that the mushrooms are well arranged. Close the lid—Cook for about 4-5 hours on low. When cooked, serve in the slow cooker to keep warm or transfer them into a serving platter.

Nutrition (per Serving): Calories 142 Fat 9 g Protein 10.7 g   Carbs 6.2 g

Etouffee

Prep Time: 15 minutes | Cooking Time: 7 hours

Ingredients (6 Servings):

- 1½ lb. peeled and deveined raw shrimp
- 1½ lb. quartered scallops
- 4 tbsp olive oil
- 2 medium onions diced
- 8 scallions, chopped
- 2 celery stalks, diced
- 2 diced small green bell peppers
- 3 minced garlic cloves
- 20 oz diced tomatoes
- 6 tbsp tomato paste
- ¾ tsp dried basil
- ¾ tsp dried thyme
- ¾ tsp dried oregano
- 1/3 tsp cayenne pepper
- 3 tsp almond meal
- 1½ tbsp cold water
- Hot sauce

Directions:

Combine the olive oil and onion in the slow cooker. Add the scallions, bell pepper, and celery. Mix well. Cook within 30 minutes, high. Add the tomato paste and garlic—cover and cook for 15 minutes on high. Add the tomatoes, cayenne, thyme, oregano, basil, and salt—Cook within 6 hours on low. Add the shrimp and scallops. Set heat to high, cover, and cook for 15 minutes. Combine the almond meal and water. Add the mixture in your slow cooker for about 6 minutes to thicken. Add a few drops of hot sauce and stir.

Nutrition (per Serving): Calories 247 Protein 19 g Fat 1.3 g Carbs 6.2 g

Poached Salmon

Prep Time: 15 minutes | Cooking Time: 1 hour

Ingredients (8 Servings):

- 2 tbsp butter
- 1 sliced large sweet onion
- 3 cup water
- 2 tbsp lemon juice
- 2 sprigs fresh dill
- 8 salmon fillets
- 2 quartered lemons

Directions:

Butter the inside of the slow cooker. Place the onion rings on the bottom in a single layer.

Slowly pour the water into the slow cooker— Cook within a half an hour on high.

On top of the onion slices, place salmon fillets— season with the fresh dill, salt, and some lemon juice. Cover the cooker and cook for 30 minutes on high or until the salmon is no longer pink on the outside. Drain the fillets very well and serve with the lemon wedges.

Nutrition (per Serving): Calories 100 Protein 40.1 g   Fat 3.4 g Carbs 3.75 g

Italian Fish Soup

Prep Time: 15 minutes | Cooking Time: 4 hours

Ingredients (3 Servings):

- ½ cup chicken broth
- ¼ cup dry red wine or chicken broth
- 1 lb. chopped tomatoes
- 2 chopped small onion
- 1½ minced garlic cloves garlic

- ½ tsp dried oregano
- ½ tsp dried sage
- ½ tsp dried rosemary leaves
- 1/8 tsp red pepper, crushed
- ¾ lb. assorted skinless fish fillets
- 3 oz peeled and deveined shrimp
- 3 slices Italian bread, toasted
- 1 halved clove garlic

Directions:

In a slow cooker, mix all the ingredients except for the seafood, bread, and halved garlic cloves. Cook on high for 4 hours. In the last 15 minutes, add the seafood—season with salt and pepper. In the meantime, rub the garlic cloves on the bread. Place bread into soup bowls and ladle the soup on top. Serve piping hot.

Nutrition (per Serving): Calories 132.2 Fat 3.3 g Carbs 18.9 g Protein 7.6 g

Taco Wraps

Prep Time: 5 minutes | Cooking Time: 2 hours

Ingredients (6 Servings):

- 1 lb. Mahi-Mahi, wild-caught
- ½ cup cherry tomatoes
- 1 green bell pepper
- 1/4 medium red onion
- ½ tsp garlic powder
- 1 tsp chipotle pepper
- ½ tsp dried oregano
- 1 tsp cumin
- 3 tbsp avocado oil
- 1/4 cup chicken stock
- 1 avocado, diced
- 1 ½ cup sour cream
- 6 large lettuce leaves

Directions:

Grease a slow cooker with oil, place fish in it and then pour in chicken stock.

Stir together garlic powder, chipotle pepper, oregano, and cumin and then season fish with half of this mixture. Layer fish with tomatoes, pepper, and onion, season with remaining spice mixture, and shut with lid. Plugin the slow cooker, then cook fish for 2 hours at a high heat setting or until cooked. When done, evenly spoon fish among lettuce, top with avocado and sour cream, and serve.

Nutrition (per Serving): Calories 193.6 Fat 12g Protein 17g Carbs 5g Fiber 3g

Shrimp Scampi

Prep Time: 5 minutes | Cooking Time: 2 H 30 minutes

Ingredients (4 Servings):

- 1 lb. wild-caught shrimps, peeled & deveined
- 1 tbsp minced garlic
- 1 tsp red pepper flakes
- 2 tbsp chopped parsley
- 2 tbsp avocado oil
- 2 tbsp unsalted butter
- ½ cup white wine
- 1 tbsp lemon juice
- ¼ cup vegetable broth

Directions:

Place all the ingredients except for shrimps in a 6-quart slow cooker and whisk until combined. Add shrimps and stir until evenly coated and shut with lid.

Cook in the slow cooker for 1 hour and 30 minutes to 2 hours and 30 minutes at low heat setting or until cooked. Then serve.

Nutrition (per Serving): Calories 234 Fat 14.7g Protein 23.3g Carbs 2.1g

Shrimp Tacos

Prep Time: 5 minutes | Cooking Time: 3 hours

Ingredients (6 Servings):

- 1 lb. medium shrimp, peeled and tails off
- 12-oz fire-roasted tomatoes, diced
- 1 green bell pepper, chopped
- ½ cup chopped white onion
- 1 tsp minced garlic
- ½ tsp red chili powder
- ½ tsp cumin
- ¼ tsp cayenne pepper
- 3 tbsp avocado oil
- ½ cup salsa
- 3 tbsp chopped cilantro
- 1 ½ cup sour cream
- 2 avocados, diced

Directions:

Rinse shrimps, layer into a 6-quarts slow cooker, and drizzle with oil.

Add tomatoes, stir until mixed, then add peppers and remaining ingredients except for sour cream and avocado and stir until combined. Plugin the slow cooker, shut with lid, and cook for 2 to 3 hours at low heat setting or 1 hour and 30 minutes at high heat setting or until shrimps turn pink. When done, serve shrimps with avocado and sour cream.

Nutrition (per Serving): Calories 369 Fat 27.5g Protein 21.2g Carbs 9.2g Fiber 5g

Braised Squid with Tomatoes and Fennel

Prep Time: 20 minutes | Cooking Time: 4 hours

Ingredients (2 Servings):

- 1 ½ cups clam juice
- 1 can plum tomatoes
- ½ fennel bulb, minced
- 4 tbsp all-purpose flour
- 1 lb. squid in 1-inch pieces

Directions:

Add chopped onions, fennel, and garlic to the flameproof insert of a slow cooker and cook on a stove in medium heat for about 5 minutes. Whisk in flour and tomato paste until thoroughly mixed, then add the clam juice, tomatoes, 1 tsp salt, and pepper. Boil for about 2 minutes.

Transfer to the slow cooker, cover, and cook for 3 hours on low. Uncover, add the squid and mix well—Cook for another 1 hour.

Nutrition (per Serving): Calories 210 Fat 25g Carbs 6g Protein 29g

Seafood Stir-Fry Soup

Prep Time: 30 minutes | Cooking Time: 3 H 10 minutes

Ingredients (2 Servings):

- 7.25 oz low-carb udon noodle, beef flavor
- ½ lb. shrimp
- ¼ lb. scallops
- 3 cups fish broth
- 1 carrot, shredded

Directions:

Add all ingredients except noodles, shrimp, and scallops to the slow cooker. Include seasonings such as garlic, ginger, salt, and pepper to taste. Add vinegar, soy sauce, and fish sauce, ½ tbsp each. Stir to mix well. Cook on high for 2-3 hours. Add udon noodles, shrimp, and scallops. Cook on high for additional 10-15 minutes.

Nutrition (per Serving): Calories 266 Fat 19g Carbs 8g Protein 27.5g

Shrimp Fajita Soup

Prep Time: 20 minutes | Cooking Time: 2 hours

Ingredients (2 Servings):

- ½ lb. shrimp
- 30 oz vegetable broth
- 1 tbsp fajita seasoning
- ½ bell pepper, sliced or diced

Directions:

Put all the listed items except the shrimp in the slow cooker. Add onion slices to taste and stir to mix well. Cook on high for 2 hours. Add the shrimp and cook for additional 5-15 minutes.

Nutrition (per Serving): Calories 165 Fat 7.3g Carbs 3.7g Protein 15.9g

Fish and Tomatoes

Prep Time: 7 minutes | Cooking Time: 3 hours

Ingredients (2 Servings):

- ½ bell pepper, sliced
- ½ lb. cod
- 1/8 cup low-sodium broth
- 6 oz diced tomatoes
- ½ tbsp rosemary

Directions:

Put all the listed fixing except the fish in the slow cooker. Add garlic, salt, and pepper to taste.

Season fish with your favorite seasoning and place other ingredients in the pot. Cook for 3 hours on low.

Nutrition (per Serving): Calories 204 Fat 16.8g Carbs 5g Protein 25.3g

Hot Crab Dip

Prep Time: 10 minutes |Cooking Time: 3 hours

Ingredients (2 Servings):

- 1/8 cup grated Parmesan cheese
- 1/4 package cream cheese, softened
- 1/8 cup mayonnaise
- 6 oz crabmeat, drained and flaked

Directions:

In a slow cooker, combine the ingredients. Stir, cover, and cook on low for 2-3 hours. Serve.

Nutrition (per Serving): Calories 190 Fat 16g Carbs 3g Protein 8g

Cod and Zoodles Stew

Prep Time: 5 minutes | Cooking Time: 2 hours

Ingredients (2 Servings):

- 2 zucchini, made into zoodles
- 1/8 cup low-sodium broth
- ½ bell pepper, diced
- ½ lb. sablefish or any whitefish
- 14 oz diced tomatoes

Directions:

Prepare seasonings: onion, garlic, pepper, and salt to taste. Place all the ingredients in the slow cooker and add the prepared seasonings—cook on high for 2 hours.

Nutrition (per Serving): Calories 209 Fat 20g Carbs 3g Protein 15g

Slow-Cooked Tilapia

Prep Time: 10 minutes | Cooking Time: 4 hours

Ingredients (2 Servings):

- 1 lb. tilapia, sliced
- ½ fresh lemon, juiced
- ½ cup mayonnaise
- 1 garlic clove, chopped

Directions:

Whisk mayo and lemon juice in a bowl. Add some chopped garlic. Spread the mixture on all sides of the tilapia. Cook on low for 3-4 hours.

Nutrition (per Serving): Calories 189 Fat 18g Carbs 4g Protein 22g

Lemony Salmon

Prep Time: 10 minutes | Cooking Time: 2 hours

Ingredients (2 Servings):

- 1 tsp olive oil
- 2 lb. salmon
- 1 lemon, sliced
- A handful of fresh dill

Directions:

Rub salmon with the oil, salt, pepper, garlic, and fresh dill. Put the salmon in the slow cooker and place lemon slices on top. Cook on high for 1 hour or low for 2.

Nutrition (per Serving): Calories 159 Fat 16g Carbs 2g Protein 37g

Crab Zucchini Casserole

Prep Time: 20 minutes | Cooking Time: 5 hours

Ingredients (2 Servings):

- ¼ cup heavy cream
- 2 zucchini squash
- 2 oz cream cheese
- 4 oz crab meat
- 1 tsp butter

Directions:

Spiralize zucchini squash on wide ribbons and season with salt. Place the ribbons in a steamer basket and heat for 5 to 7 minutes. Put all ingredients in a slow cooker, including seasonings such as garlic, onions. Put the zucchini spirals on top—Cook within 5 hours on low.

Nutrition (per Serving): Calories 162.6 Fat 11.9g Carbs 2.8g Protein 7.2g

Lobster Bisque

Prep Time: 20 minutes | Cooking Time: 6 hours

Ingredients (2 Servings):

- 1 1/3 lobster tails, fan parts cut out
- 2/3 tsp Worcestershire sauce
- 2 tbsp tomato paste
- 2/3 cup lobster stock
- 2/3 cup heavy cream

Directions:

Enhance the broth: slowly add broth to an onion-garlic sauté. Put the broth plus all the other listed fixing except the heavy cream in the slow cooker, including desired spices to taste (paprika, thyme, black pepper)—Cook within 6 hours on low. Once cooked add heavy cream and serve.

Nutrition (per Serving): Calories 400 Fat 30g Carbs 7g Protein 23g

Clam Chowder

Prep Time: 15 minutes | Cooking Time: 6 hours

Ingredients (6 Servings):

- 20-oz wild-caught baby clams, with juice
- ½ cup chopped scallion
- ½ cup chopped celery
- 1 tsp dried thyme
- 1 tbsp avocado oil
- 2 cups coconut cream, full-fat
- 2 cups chicken broth

Directions:

Grease a 6-quart slow cooker with oil, then add ingredients and stir until mixed.

Plugin the slow cooker, shut with lid, and cook for 4 to 6 hours at low heat setting or until cooked. Serve straight away.

Nutrition (per Serving): Calories 357 Fat 28.9g Protein 15.2g Carbs 8.9g Fiber 2g

Soy Steamed Pompano

Prep Time: 5 minutes | Cooking Time: 1 hour

Ingredients (4 Servings):

- 1 wild-caught whole pompano, gutted and scaled
- 1 bunch scallion, diced
- 1 bunch cilantro, chopped
- 3 tsp minced garlic
- 1 tbsp grated ginger
- 1 tbsp swerve sweetener
- ¼ cup of soy sauce
- ¼ cup white wine
- ¼ cup sesame oil

Directions:

Place scallions in a 6-quart slow cooker and top with fish. Whisk together remaining ingredients, except for cilantro, and pour the mixture all over the fish. Plugin the slow cooker, shut with lid, and cook for 1 hour at high heat or until cooked.

Garnish with cilantro and serve.

Nutrition (per Serving): Calories 202.5 Fat 24.2g Protein 22.7g Carbs 4g

Vietnamese Catfish

Prep Time: 5 minutes | Cooking Time: 6 hours

Ingredients (3 Servings):

- 1 fillet of wild-caught catfish, cut into bite-size pieces
- 2 scallion, chopped
- 2 red chilies, chopped

- 1 tbsp grated ginger
- ½ cup swerve sweetener
- 3 tbsp avocado oil
- ¼ cup fish sauce, unsweetened

Directions:

Put a small saucepan over medium heat, put the sweetener, and cook until it melts.

Then add scallion, chilies, ginger, and fish sauce and stir until mixed. Transfer this mixture in a 4-quart slow cooker, add fish and toss until coated. Plugin the slow cooker, shut with lid, and cook for 6 hours at low heat setting until cooked. Drizzle with avocado oil and serve straight away.

Nutrition (per Serving): Calories 110.7 Fat 8g Protein 9.4g Carbs 0.3g Fiber 0.2g

Chili Shrimps

Prep Time: 15 minutes | Cooking Time: 2 hours

Ingredients (6 Servings):

- 1 lb. peeled and deveined raw shrimps
- 1 lb. tomatoes, fire-roasted
- 2 tbsp spicy salsa
- ½ cup chopped bell pepper
- ½ tsp cumin
- ½ tsp cayenne pepper
- ½ tsp minced garlic
- 2 tbsp chopped cilantro
- 2 tbsp olive oil

Directions:

Drizzle the slow cooker with a generous amount of olive oil. Place the shrimps at the bottom of it. Put the rest of the fixing into the slow cooker. Cook on high for 2 hours.

Nutrition (per Serving): Calories 185 Fat 6.7 g Carbs 5.2 g Protein 28.4 g

Fennel Flavored Fish Stew

Prep Time: 15 minutes | Cooking Time: 6 hours

Ingredients (4 Servings):

- 1 lb. firm fish fillets, chopped
- ½ qt clam juice
- ¼ cup dry white wine
- 2 peeled and chopped medium tomatoes
- ½ cup carrots, chopped
- ½ cup onion, chopped
- 1 minced garlic cloves
- ½ tbsp minced orange zest
- ½ tsp lightly crushed fennel seeds
- 1/8 cup parsley chopped

Directions:

In a slow cooker, mix all the ingredients, except for the fish fillets, and parsley. Cook on low for 6 hours. Add the fish within the last 15 minutes. Add the parsley and stir to distribute—season with salt and pepper before serving.

Nutrition (per Serving): Calories 342 Fat 8.2 g Carbs 21 g Protein 36g

Spicy Shrimps

Prep Time: 10 minutes | Cooking Time: 3 hours

Ingredients (2 Servings):

- ¼ lb. shrimp, shelled and deveined
- 1 tsp olive oil
- 1 onion, diced
- 5 cloves of garlic, minced
- 1 tsp red pepper flakes
- 1 can fire-roasted tomatoes
- 1 tbsp Italian parsley

Directions:

Set the slow cooker to high heat and heat the oil. Sauté the onion and garlic for 2 minutes.

Add the pepper flakes and tomatoes—season with black pepper and salt. Add the shrimps. Adjust the heat setting to low and cook for 2 or 3 hours. Garnish with parsley.

Nutrition (per Serving): Calories 134 Carbs 3.41 g Protein 13.99g Fat 3.44 g

Shrimp with Spaghetti Squash

Prep Time: 10 minutes | Cooking Time: 2 H 20 minutes

Ingredients (4 Servings):

- 3 lb. spaghetti squash, cut lengthwise and seeds removed
- ¾-lb. shrimp, shelled and deveined
- 1 cup fish broth
- 2 tsp lemon-garlic seasoning
- 1 onion, chopped
- 1 tbsp butter

Directions:

Pour broth in the slow cooker and add the lemon-garlic seasoning, onion, and butter. Place the spaghetti squash inside the slow cooker and cook on high for 2 hours until soft.

Add the shrimps and cook for 20 more minutes on high.

Nutrition (per Serving): Calories 239 Carbs 16.79g Protein 21.19g Fat 6.28g

Tuna and White Beans

Prep Time: 10 minutes | Cooking Time: 5 hours

Ingredients (4 Servings):

- 3 cans white tuna, drained and flaked

- 1 lb. white beans, soaked overnight and drained
- 2 cups chopped tomatoes
- 4 tbsp olive oil
- 1 clove of garlic, minced
- 4 cups of water
- 2 sprigs of basil

Directions:

Set the slow cooker to high heat and add oil. Sauté the garlic for 2 minutes and add water.

Stir in the beans—Cook within 5 hours on low. Add in the tomatoes, tuna, and basil—season with salt and pepper to taste. Continue cooking on high for 15 minutes.

Nutrition (per Serving): Calories 764 Carbs 12.05g Protein 62.84g Fat 25.43g

Slow cooker Swordfish Steaks

Prep Time: 10 minutes | Cooking Time: 2 hours

Ingredients (4 Servings):

- 4 swordfish steaks
- ½ cup olive oil
- ¼ cup lemon juice
- ½ tsp Worcestershire sauce
- 1 tsp cayenne pepper powder
- ¼ tsp paprika

Directions:

Place the swordfish steaks in the slow cooker. Pour the other ingredients over the swordfish steaks. Close the lid and cook on high for 2 hours. Serve.

Nutrition (per Serving): Calories 659 Carbs 1.63g Protein 469g Fat 50.78g

SALT & PEPPER *the list of ingredient list do not indicate the amount of salt and pepper: you can add approximately a teaspoon of salt and, in if you like it, 1/2 teaspoon of pepper for each recipe*

CHAPTER 5: POULTRY

Sour Cream Chicken

Prep Time: 15 minutes | Cooking Time: 6 hours

Ingredients (4 Servings):

- 2 lb. chicken breast
- 1 cup sour cream
- ½ cup chicken stock
- 1 can diced green chilies and tomatoes
- 1 batch of taco seasoning

Directions:

Put all the items to the slow cooker. Cook on low for 6 hours. Divide onto plates and serve.

Nutrition (per Serving): Calories 561 Fat 27 g Protein 69 g Carbs 3 g

Lemon Thyme Chicken

Prep Time: 15 minutes | Cooking Time: 4 hours

Ingredients (4 Servings):

- 2 lb. whole chicken
- 10-12 cloves of garlic
- 2 sliced lemons

- ½ tsp ground pepper
- 1 tsp thyme

Directions:

Arrange the lemon and garlic on the base of a slow cooker. Mix the spices and use them to season the chicken. Put the chicken in the slow cooker. Cook on Low within 4 hours. Remove, let it cool within 15 minutes, and then serve.

Nutrition (per Serving): Calories 440 Fat 15 g Carbs 1 g Protein 62 g

Balsamic Oregano Chicken

Prep Time: 15 minutes | Cooking Time: 4 hours

Ingredients (6 Servings):

- 6 pieces boneless, skinless chicken
- 2 cans diced tomatoes
- 1 large onion, thinly sliced
- 4 cloves garlic
- ½ cup balsamic vinegar
- 1 tbsp olive oil
- 1 tbsp dried oregano
- 1 tsp dried basil
- ½ tsp thyme

Directions:

Combine all the fixings except for the chicken in a small bowl. Mix them thoroughly. Put the chicken inside the slow cooker, then pour the remaining ingredients over the top. Cook on high for 4 hours.

Nutrition (per Serving): Calories 370 Fat 6 g Carbs 75 g Protein 3 g

Chicken Breast with Artichoke Stuffing

Prep Time: 15 minutes | Cooking Time: 4 hours

Ingredients (4 Servings):

- 4 boneless, skinless chicken breasts
- 2 cups finely chopped spinach
- ½ cup chopped roasted red peppers
- ¼ cup sliced black olives
- 1 cup chopped canned artichoke hearts
- 3 oz reduced-fat feta cheese
- 1 tsp dried oregano
- 1 tsp garlic powder
- 1 ½ cups low-sodium chicken broth

Directions:

Cut deep in the center of the chicken and season it with salt and pepper. In a small bowl, combine the garlic, feta, oregano, peppers, spinach, and artichoke hearts. Stuff the chicken with the artichoke mixture and put it into the slow cooker. Cook within low for 4 hours.

Nutrition (per Serving): Calories 202 Fat 7 g Carbs 8g Protein 15 g

Chipotle BBQ Chicken

Prep Time: 20 minutes | Cooking Time: 8 hours

Ingredients (5 Servings):

- 1 14-oz boneless chicken breasts, skin removed
- 1 14-oz boneless chicken thighs, skin removed
- 2 tbsp chipotle Tabasco sauce
- 1 cup tomato sauce
- ½ cup apple cider vinegar
- 1 onion, chopped
- 3 tbsp unsalted butter
- 2 tbsp yellow mustard
- ¼ tsp garlic powder
- ½ cup water

Directions:

Put all ingredients in a slow cooker. Stir everything so that the chicken is coated with the sauce. Cook within 8 hours, low. Serve.

Nutrition (per Serving): Calories 482 Carbs 13g Protein 50g Fat 18.7g

Spicy Shredded Chicken Wraps

Prep Time: 15 minutes | Cooking Time: 10 hours

Ingredients (8 Servings):

- 4 chicken breast, skin and bones removed
- 1 cup tomato salsa
- 2 tsp onion powder
- 1 can dice green chilies
- 1 tbsp Tabasco sauce
- 2 tbsp freshly squeezed lime juice
- 8 large heads iceberg lettuce, rinsed

Directions:

Put the chicken breast in the slow cooker. Pour over the tomato salsa, onion powder, green chilies, Tabasco sauce, and lime juice. Season with pepper and salt to taste. Close the lid and cook for 10 hours. Shred the chicken meat using a fork. Take on top of lettuce leaves. Garnish with sour cream, tomatoes, or avocado slices if needed.

Nutrition (per Serving): Calories 96 Carbs 8g Protein 13 g Fat 0g

Orange Chicken

Prep Time: 10 minutes | Cooking Time: 7 hours

Ingredients (6 Servings):

- 1 lb. chicken breasts, skinless & boneless
- 2 tbsp soy sauce
- 1 cup sweet orange marmalade
- 1 cup BBQ sauce

Directions:

Add all ingredients into the cooking pot and stir well. Cover and cook on Low for 7 hours. Remove chicken from pot and shred using a fork, return shredded chicken to the pot and stir well. Serve.

Nutrition (per Serving): Calories 256 Fat 5.7 g Carbs 38g Protein 22.2 g

Delicious BBQ Chicken

Prep Time: 10 minutes | Cooking Time: 4 hours

Ingredients (8 Servings):

- 3 lb. chicken breasts, skinless & boneless
- 2 tbsp brown sugar
- 1 tbsp Worcestershire sauce
- 2 tbsp olive oil
- 1 onion, grated
- 1 cup BBQ sauce

Directions:

Add all ingredients into the cooking pot and stir well. Cover and cook on High for 4 hours. Remove chicken from pot and shred using a fork, return shredded chicken to the pot and stir well. Serve.

Nutrition (per Serving): Calories 422 Fat 14.5 g Carbs 20.2 Protein 49.3 g

Parmesan Chicken Rice

Prep Time: 10 minutes | Cooking Time: 4 hours

Ingredients (6 Servings):

- 4 chicken breasts, skinless & boneless
- ¼ cup parmesan cheese, grated
- 1 cup of rice
- 2 cup milk
- 20 oz can cream of chicken soup

Directions:

Season chicken with pepper and salt and place into the cooking pot.

Mix together rice, milk, and soup and pour over chicken and top with parmesan cheese.

Cover and cook on High for 4 hours. Remove chicken from pot and chop, return chicken to the pot and stir well. Serve and enjoy.

Nutrition (per Serving): Calories 453 Fat 16.7 g Carbs 35.6 g Sugar 3.8 g Protein 38.2

Queso Chicken Tacos

Prep Time: 10 minutes | Cooking Time: 4 hours

Ingredients (8 Servings):

- 2 lb. chicken breasts, boneless & skinless
- 1 1/2 cups Mexican cheese dip
- 10 oz can Rotel (or diced tomatoes)
- 1 oz taco seasoning

Directions:

Add all ingredients into the cooking pot and stir well. Cover and cook on Low for 4-6 hours. Remove chicken from pot and shred using a fork, return shredded chicken to the pot and stir well. Serve and enjoy.

Nutrition (per Serving): Calories 349 Fat 17.8 g Carbs 4.7 g Sugar 0.9 g Protein 39 g

Easy Mexican Chicken

Prep Time: 10 minutes | Cooking Time: 6 hours

Ingredients (6 Servings):

- 2 lb. chicken breasts, boneless & skinless
- 1/3 cup chicken stock

- 1 oz taco seasoning
- 2 cups salsa

Directions:

Add all ingredients into the cooking pot and stir well. Cover and cook on Low for 6 hours. Remove chicken from pot and shred using a fork, return shredded chicken to the pot and stir well. Serve and enjoy.

Nutrition (per Serving): Calories 402 Fat 12 g Carbs 16.2 g Protein 51.7 g

Mushroom Chicken

Prep Time: 10 minutes | Cooking Time: 6 hours

Ingredients (4 Servings):

- 4 chicken thighs, bone-in & skin-on
- 1 tsp garlic, minced
- 1 tsp grainy mustard
- 8 oz mushrooms, sliced
- 10 oz cream of mushroom soup

Directions:

Season chicken and place it into the cooking pot. Mix together remaining ingredients and pour over chicken. Cover and cook on Low for 6 hours. Serve and enjoy.

Nutrition (per Serving): Calories 184 Fat 13 g Carbs 2.7 g Protein 15 g

Herbs Chicken Breasts

Prep Time: 10 minutes | Cooking Time: 5 hours

Ingredients (6 Servings):

- 6 chicken breasts, boneless & skinless
- 1/3 cup dry white wine
- 1 garlic clove, crushed
- 1 tsp thyme, chopped
- 2 tsp fresh oregano, chopped

Directions:

Season chicken with pepper and salt and place into the cooking pot. Mix together remaining ingredients and pour over chicken. Cover and cook on Low for 5 hours. Serve and enjoy.

Nutrition (per Serving): Calories 131 Fat 2.9 g Carbs 1 g Protein 22 g

Balsamic Chicken

Prep Time: 10 minutes | Cooking Time: 4 hours

Ingredients (8 Servings):

- 4 chicken breasts, boneless & skinless
- ½ tsp thyme
- 1 tsp dried rosemary
- 1 tsp dried oregano
- 2 tbsp olive oil
- ½ cup balsamic vinegar
- 2 garlic cloves
- 1 onion, sliced
- 20 oz can tomato, diced

Directions:

Season chicken and place into the cooking pot. Mix together remaining ingredients and pour over chicken. Cover and cook on High for 4 hours. Serve and enjoy.

Nutrition (per Serving): Calories 191 Fat 5.8 g Carbs 26.1 g Protein 17 g

Creamy Chicken Pasta

Prep Time: 10 minutes | Cooking Time: 6 hours

Ingredients (6 Servings):

- 3 chicken breasts, boneless & skinless
- 1 lb. pasta, cooked
- 2 cups cheddar cheese, shredded
- 1 cup sour cream
- ½ onion, diced

- 1 cup mushrooms, sliced
- ½ tsp dried thyme
- ½ cup chicken broth
- 20 oz can cream of chicken soup

Directions:

Add chicken, soup, onions, mushrooms, thyme, pepper, and broth into the cooking pot and stir well. Cover and cook on LOW for 6 hours. Remove chicken from pot and shred using a fork, return shredded chicken to the pot and stir well. Stir in cheddar cheese, penne, and sour cream. Serve.

Nutrition (per Serving): Calories 442 Fat 23.6 g Carbs 24g Protein 33g

Chicken Fajita Pasta

Prep Time: 10 minutes | Cooking Time: 6 hours

Ingredients (6 Servings):

- 2 chicken breasts, skinless & boneless
- 1 ½ cup cheddar cheese, shredded
- 14 oz penne pasta, cooked
- 2 cups chicken broth
- 10 oz can tomato, diced
- 2 tsp garlic, minced
- 1 bell peppers, diced
- ½ onion, diced
- 2 tbsp taco seasoning

Directions:

Add all ingredients except cheese and pasta into the cooking pot and stir well. Cover and cook on Low for 6 hours. Stir in cheese and pasta. Serve.

Nutrition (per Serving): Calories 347 Fat 12 g Carbs 42g Protein 19.3 g

Chicken Breast

Prep Time: 10 minutes | Cooking Time: 3 hours

Ingredients (4 Servings):

- 4 chicken breasts, skinless and boneless
- 1/8 tsp paprika
- 1 tbsp butter
- ¼ cup chicken broth
- ¼ tsp onion powder
- ¼ tsp garlic powder
- ½ tsp dried parsley

Directions:

In a small bowl, mix together paprika, onion powder, garlic powder, parsley, pepper, and salt.

Rub chicken breasts with a spice mixture from both the sides. Add broth and butter to the cooking pot and stir to combine. Add chicken to the cooking pot. Cover and cook on LOW for 3 hours. Serve and enjoy.

Nutrition (per Serving): Calories 137 Fat 5.8 g Carbs 0.4 g Protein 23 g

Asian Chicken

Prep Time: 10 minutes | Cooking Time: 6 hours

Ingredients (4 Servings):

- 4 chicken breasts, skinless and boneless
- ½ cup soy sauce
- 1 tbsp ginger, minced
- 2 garlic cloves, chopped
- 1 onion, chopped
- 2 tbsp sesame seeds
- 1/3 cup rice vinegar
- 1/3 cup honey

Directions:

Add chicken into the cooking pot. Add ginger, garlic, and onion on top of the chicken.

Add vinegar, honey, and soy sauce to the cooking pot. Season with pepper and salt.

Cover and cook on LOW for 6 hours.

Shred chicken using a fork and stir well. Serve.

Nutrition (per Serving): Calories 205 Fat 2.3 g Carbs 23 g Protein 26.1 g

Tasty Chicken Casserole

Prep Time: 10 minutes | Cooking Time: 8 hours

Ingredients (6 Servings):

- 3 chicken breasts, boneless & skinless
- 1 cup chicken stock
- 8 oz can cream of chicken soup
- 12 oz can corn kernels, drained
- 1 ½ cup cheddar cheese, shredded
- 1 cup cooked rice
- 1 onion, chopped

Directions:

Add chicken into the cooking pot. Add chopped onion over chicken. In a bowl, stir together stock and soup and pour over the chicken. Cover and cook on LOW for 8 hours. Remove chicken from cooking pot and shred using a fork. Return shredded chicken to the cooking pot along with corn, cheese, and rice. Stir well. Serve.

Nutrition (per Serving): Calories 186 Fat 11.6g Carbs 3g Protein 23.2 g

Chicken Barley

Prep Time: 10 minutes | Cooking Time: 4 hours

Ingredients (4 Servings):

- 1 lb. chicken breasts, skinless and boneless, cut in half
- 3/4 cup whole barley
- 1 tsp Italian herbs

- 1 tbsp lemon juice
- 2 tbsp green onion, chopped
- 1/3 cup olives
- 1 lemon zest, grated
- 1 onion, sliced
- 1 cup chicken stock
- ½ cup bell pepper, diced
- 3 tomatoes, chopped

Directions:

Add all ingredients except olives and orzo into the cooking pot and stir well. Cover and cook on Low for 4 hours. Stir in olives and orzo and cook for 30 minutes more. Serve and enjoy.

Nutrition (per Serving): Calories 273 Fat 10.6 g Carbs 5g Protein 36.4 g

Garlic Herb Roasted Pepper Chicken

Prep Time: 10 minutes | Cooking Time: 4 hours

Ingredients (6 Servings):

- 2 lb. chicken thighs, skinless and boneless
- 1 cup roasted red peppers, chopped
- ½ cup chicken or vegetable stock
- 1 cup olives
- 1 tsp dried thyme
- 1 tsp oregano
- 1 tbsp capers
- 3 garlic cloves, minced
- 1 onion, sliced
- 1 tbsp olive oil

Directions:

Add all ingredients into the cooking pot and stir well. Cover and cook on Low for 4 hours. Stir well and serve.

Nutrition (per Serving): Calories 424 Fat 26.1 g Carbs 2 g Protein 37.7 g

Slow Cook Turkey Breast

Prep Time: 10 minutes | Cooking Time: 4 hours

Ingredients (6 Servings):

- 4 lb. turkey breast
- 2 tbsp fresh lemon juice
- ½ cup sun-dried tomatoes, chopped
- ½ cup olives, chopped
- 3 tbsp flour
- 3/4 cup chicken stock
- 3 garlic cloves, chopped
- 1 tsp dried oregano
- 1 onion, chopped

Directions:

Add turkey breast, garlic, oregano, lemon juice, sun-dried tomatoes, olives, onion, pepper, and salt to the cooking pot. Pour half stock over turkey. Cover and cook on Low for 4 hours. Whisk together remaining stock and flour and add into the cooking pot and stir well, cover, and cook on Low for 30 minutes more.

Serve and enjoy.

Nutrition (per Serving): Calories 612 Fat 26.5 g Carbs 1.8 g Protein 92.7

Simple Chicken & Mushrooms

Prep Time: 10 minutes | Cooking Time: 6 hours

Ingredients (2 Servings):

- 2 chicken breasts, skinless and boneless
- 1 cup mushrooms, sliced
- ½ tsp thyme, dried
- 2 onion, sliced
- 1 cup chicken stock

Directions:

Add all ingredients into the cooking pot and stir well. Cover and cook on Low for 6 hours. Stir well and serve.

Nutrition (per Serving): Calories 133 Fat 2.3 g Carbs 1.9 g Protein 24.3g

Lemony Herbs Chicken

Prep Time: 10 minutes | Cooking Time: 4 hours

Ingredients (4 Servings):

- 18 oz chicken breasts, skinless, boneless, and cut into pieces
- 3/4 cup chicken broth
- 2 tbsp olive oil
- 2 tbsp butter
- 3 tbsp lemon juice
- 1/8 tsp dried thyme
- 1/4 tsp dried basil
- 1 tsp dried oregano
- 1 tsp dried parsley
- 3 tbsp rice flour

Directions:

In a bowl, toss chicken with rice flour. Add butter and olive oil in a cooking pot. Add chicken to the cooking pot and cook until brown.

Add remaining ingredients on top of the chicken. Cover and cook on Low for 4 hours. Serve and enjoy.

Nutrition (per Serving): Calories 233 Fat 7.9 g Carbs 1 g Protein 32.7 g

Creamy Chicken Curry

Prep Time: 10 minutes | Cooking Time: 6 hours

Ingredients (6 Servings):

- 1 ½ lb. chicken thighs, boneless

- ½ cup chicken broth
- 3 potatoes, peeled and cut into 1-inch pieces
- 10 oz can coconut milk
- 2 tbsp brown sugar
- ½ tsp red pepper, crushed
- ½ tsp coriander, crushed
- 3 tbsp curry powder
- 3 tbsp fresh ginger, chopped

Directions:

Add all ingredients into the cooking pot and stir well. Cover and cook on Low for 6 hours. Stir well and serve.

Nutrition (per Serving): Calories 449 Fat 27.2 g Carbs 18g Protein 32.1 g

Taco Chicken

Prep Time: 10 minutes | Cooking Time: 6 hours

Ingredients (8 Servings):

- 1 lb. chicken breasts, skinless and boneless
- 2 tbsp taco seasoning
- 1 cup chicken broth

Directions:

Add all ingredients into the cooking pot and stir well. Cover instant pot aura with lid. Select slow cook mode and cook on Low for 6 hours. Remove chicken from pot and shred using a fork, return shredded chicken to the pot. Stir well and serve.

Nutrition (per Serving): Calories 118 Fat 4.7 g Carbs 0.5 g Protein 17.3

Buttered Chicken

Prep Time: 10 minutes | Cooking Time: 5 hours

Ingredients (6 Servings):

- 1 lb. chicken thighs, boneless and skinless
- 1 lb. chicken breasts, boneless and skinless
- 1 tbsp ginger paste
- 1 tbsp garam masala
- 1 tbsp curry powder
- 1/3 cup heavy whipping cream
- 2 tbsp butter
- 1/4 cup tomato paste
- 1/2 cup chicken broth

Directions:

Cut chicken into the cooking pot. Pour remaining ingredients except whipping cream over chicken and stir well. Cover and cook on Low for 5 hours. Stir in cream and serve.

Nutrition (per Serving): Calories 427 Fat 25.3 g Carbs 4.7 g Protein 41 g

Spicy Chili Chicken

Prep Time: 10 minutes | Cooking Time: 6 hours

Ingredients (5 Servings):

- 1 lb. chicken breasts, skinless and boneless
- 1 jalapeno pepper, chopped
- 1 poblano pepper, chopped
- 10 oz can green chilies
- ½ cup dried chives
- ½ tsp paprika
- ½ tsp dried sage
- ½ tsp cumin
- 1 tsp dried oregano
- 12 oz can tomato, diced
- 2 cups of water

Directions:

Add all ingredients into the cooking pot and stir well. Cover and cook on Low for 6 hours.

Remove chicken from pot and shred using a fork, return shredded chicken to the pot. Stir well and serve.

Nutrition (per Serving): Calories 195 Fat 7.1 g Carbs 4.9 g Protein 27.9 g

Pesto and Chicken

Prep Time: 10 minutes | Cooking Time: 7 hours

Ingredients (2 Servings):

- 2 chicken breasts, skinless and boneless
- 2 cups cherry tomatoes, halved
- 3 tbsp basil pesto
- 2 cups zucchini, chopped
- 2 cups green beans, chopped

Directions:

Add all ingredients into the cooking pot and stir well. Cover and cook on Low for 7 hours. Stir well and serve.

Nutrition (per Serving): Calories 110 Fat 2.8 g Carbs 1.3 g Protein 23.4 g

Rosemary Turkey Breast

Prep Time: 10 minutes | Cooking Time: 4 hours

Ingredients (12 Servings):

- 6 lb. turkey breast, bone-in
- 4 fresh rosemary sprigs
- 1/2 cup water

Directions:

Add all ingredients into the cooking pot and stir well. Cover and cook on Low for 4 hours. Serve and enjoy.

Nutrition (per Serving): Calories 437 Fat 13.8 g Carbs 1.8 g Protein 67.7 g

Garlic Olive Chicken

Prep Time: 10 minutes | Cooking Time: 4 hours

Ingredients (6 Servings):

- 2 lb. chicken legs
- 1 tbsp capers
- 4 garlic cloves, smashed
- 3 tbsp red wine vinegar
- 1 tsp dried oregano
- 1/3 cup white wine
- 1/4 cup fresh parsley, chopped
- 1/3 cup olives, pitted

Directions:

Add all ingredients into the cooking pot and stir well. Cover and cook on Low for 4 hours. Serve.

Nutrition (per Serving): Calories 330 Fat 12 g Carbs 6.9 g Protein 43 g

Delicious Chickpea Chicken

Prep Time: 10 minutes | Cooking Time: 4 hours

Ingredients (4 Servings):

- 2 lb. chicken thighs
- 1 tsp paprika
- 2 tbsp lemon juice
- 2 tbsp olive oil
- 1 tsp garlic, minced
- 3 cups grape tomatoes, sliced
- 12 oz can chickpeas, drained and rinsed
- 1 tsp chili powder
- 1 tsp curry powder
- 1 tsp cumin
- 1 tsp oregano
- 1 tsp coriander
- 1 lemon, sliced

Directions:

Add all ingredients into the cooking pot and stir well. Cover and cook on Low for 4 hours. Serve and enjoy.

Nutrition (per Serving): Calories 638 Fat 34g Carbs 14.8 g Protein 62.3 g

Chicken Kale Soup

Prep Time: 15 minutes | Cooking Time: 6 hours

Ingredients (6 Servings):

- 1 ½ lb. chicken
- 32 oz chicken stock
- 2 tbsp olive oil
- 12 oz chicken broth
- ½ cup olive oil
- 4 oz kale
- 1/3 cups onion
- 1/4 cups lemon juice

Directions:

Cook the chicken until it achieves approximately 165°F. Do this in a pan. Shred and put it into the cooker. Process the onion, broth, and oil and put it into the cooker. Add other ingredients and mix. Low cook for 6 hours. Serve.

Nutrition (per Serving): Calories 261 Fat 15 g Protein 34 g Carbs 2 g

Creamy Italian Chicken

Prep Time: 15 minutes | Cooking Time: 6 hours

Ingredients (8 Servings):

- 1 ½ lb. chicken
- 10 oz chicken soup, cream and canned
- 2 tsp garlic powder
- 1/4 cups onion
- 2 tbsp dressing mix, Italian
- 6 oz cream cheese

Directions:

Cube the chicken. Place it in the cooker. Dice and add onions. Stir in cream cheese: mix garlic, soup, and dressing mix. Pour into the cooker. Low cook for 6 hours. Serve.

Nutrition (per Serving): Calories 255 Fat 14 g Protein 28 g Carbs 7 g

Chicken and Vegetables

Prep Time: 15 minutes | Cooking Time: 8 hours

Ingredients (8 Servings):

- 1 ½ lb. chicken that does not contain any skin or bones
- 2 cups green beans
- 1 cup chicken broth
- 2 tsp herb blend
- 2 cups carrots
- 2 onions
- 2 tbsp Worcestershire sauce

Directions:

Prepare and chop the vegetables. Put the chicken in the cooker. Add the vegetables. Pour the broth and Worcestershire sauce. Low cook for 8 hours. Serve.

Nutrition (per Serving): Calories 169 Fat 6g Protein 23 g Carbs 3g

Chicken Greek Gyros

Prep Time: 15 minutes | Cooking Time: 8 hours

Ingredients (8 Servings):

- 1 ½ lb. ground chicken
- 1 onion
- ½ cup breadcrumbs, low-carb
- 1 tsp thyme
- ¼ tsp nutmeg
- 2 tbsp olive oil
- 2 garlic cloves
- 2 eggs
- 1 lemon
- ¼ tsp cinnamon
- 8 pita bread

Toppings:

- tomato
- greek yogurt, plain
- cucumber
- lemon

Directions:

Process the garlic and onion. Mix the above with the eggs, lemon, cinnamon, salt, chicken, breadcrumbs, thyme, and nutmeg. Roll into a ball. Put in a cooker—drizzle olive oil.

Low cook for 8 hours. Once finished, put on pita and apply toppings.

Nutrition (per Serving): Calories 328 Fat 10 g Protein 28 g Carbs 25 g

Slow cooker Salsa Chicken

Prep Time: 15 minutes | Cooking Time: 4 hours

Ingredients (4 Servings):

- ½ jar salsa
- ½ can of cream mushroom soup
- 3 large boneless chicken breasts

Directions:

Lay and settle the chicken breasts inside the slow cooker. Combine in the salsa plus the mushroom soup. Set it on top of the chicken breasts. Cook on low within 4 hours, stirring occasionally, and shred once cooked, then serve.

Nutrition (per Serving): Calories 214.6 Protein 25.8g Carbs 15.3g Fat 2.6g

Pizza Casserole

Prep Time: 15 minutes | Cooking Time: 4 hours

Ingredients (3 Servings):

- 3 chicken breasts without bones
- 2 garlic cloves
- 2 tsp seasoning, Italian
- 8 oz tomato sauce
- 1 bay leaf
- ½ cup mozzarella

Directions:

Put the chicken in the cooker. Add other ingredients, except cheese. Low cook for 4 hours. After cooking, top with cheese. Serve.

Nutrition (per Serving): Calories 268 Fat 9g Protein 31 g Carbs 25g

Spicy Pulled Chicken Breast

Prep Time: 15 minutes | Cooking Time: 6 hours

Ingredients (8 Servings):

- 5 lb. chicken breasts
- 1 tsp dry oregano
- 1 tsp dry thyme
- 1 tsp dried rosemary
- 1 tsp garlic powder
- 1 tsp sweet paprika
- ½ tsp chili powder
- 3 tbsp butter
- 1 ½ cups ready-made tomato salsa
- 2 tbsp of olive oil

Directions:

Mix dry seasoning, sprinkle half on the bottom of slow cooker. Place the chicken breasts over it, sprinkle the rest of the spices. Pour the salsa over the chicken. Cover, cook on low for 6 hours. Serve.

Nutrition (per Serving): Calories 642 Carbs 8g Fat 21g Protein 84g

Roasted Chicken

Prep Time: 15 minutes | Cooking Time: 8 hours

Ingredients (6 Servings):

- 1 whole chicken (approximately 5 lb.)
- 3 garlic cloves
- 6 small onions
- 2 tbsp olive oil, for rubbing
- 2 tsp sweet paprika
- 1 tsp Cayenne pepper
- 1 tsp onion powder
- 1 tsp ground thyme
- 4 tbsp butter, cut into cubes

Directions:

Mix all dry ingredients well. Stuff the chicken belly with garlic and onions. On the bottom of the slow cooker, place four balls of aluminum foil. Set the chicken on top of the balls. Rub it generously with olive oil. Cover the chicken with seasoning, drop in butter pieces. Cover, cook on low for 8 hours.

Nutrition (per Serving): Calories 820 Carbs 1g Fat 36g Protein 117g

Easy Chicken Chili

Prep Time: 15 minutes | Cooking Time: 6 hours

Ingredients (8 Servings):

- 3 lb. boneless chicken thighs
- 8 slices bacon, chopped
- 2 tbsp butter
- 1 red onion, sliced
- 1 bell pepper, sliced
- 2 garlic cloves, minced

- 1 tsp chili powder
- 1 cup chicken broth
- ¼ cup of coconut milk
- 2 tbsp tomato paste

Directions:

Add all ingredients to the slow cooker, starting with the butter. Cover, cook on low for 6 hours.

Strip the chicken using a fork in the slow cooker. Serve.

Nutrition (per Serving): Calories 479 Carbs 3g Fat 31.5g Protein 44g

Egg Casserole with Italian Cheeses and Sun-Dried Tomatoes

Prep Time: 5 minutes | Cooking Time: 3 hours

Ingredients (8 Servings):

- 8 eggs
- 3 tbsp milk
- 3 tbsp sun-dried tomatoes, chopped
- 2 tbsp onion, minced
- 2 tbsp basil, chopped
- 1 tbsp thyme leaves
- 1 cup mixed Italian cheeses, grated

Directions:

Mix all items in a bowl. Put it inside your slow cooker and set to cook on high for 2 hours or low for 3 hours.

Nutrition (per Serving): Calories 140 Carbs 3.8g Protein 10.9g Fat 8.8g

Egg Casserole with Chayote Squash

Prep Time: 5 minutes | Cooking Time: 4 hours

Ingredients (4 Servings):

- 8 large eggs, beaten
- 2 tsp olive oil
- 1 red onion, diced
- 2 small chayote squash, grated
- ½ small red bell pepper, diced

- ¼ cup low-fat cottage cheese
- 3 tbsp milk
- ½ tsp ground cumin
- 1 ½ cup grated cheesed

Directions:

Combine all fixings in a mixing bowl. Pour into the slow cooker. Cook on high within 3 hours or on low for 4 hours.

Nutrition (per Serving): Calories 349 Carbs 2.3g Protein 28.2g Fat 23.6g

Scrambled Eggs with Smoked Salmon

Prep Time: 15 minutes | Cooking Time: 2 hours

Ingredients (6 Servings):

- ¼ lb. smoked salmon
- 10 medium eggs
- ½ cup heavy cream
- ¼ cup almond flour
- 2 tbsp butter
- fresh chives at will

Directions:

Cut the slices of salmon. Set aside for garnish. Chop the rest of the salmon into small pieces.

Take a medium bowl, whisk the eggs and cream together. Add half of the chopped chives, season eggs with salt and pepper. Add flour. Dissolve the butter over medium heat, then pour into the mixture. Grease the Slow cooker with oil or cooking spray. Add salmon pieces to the mixture, pour it into the Slow cooker. Set to cook on low within 2 hours. Garnish the dish with remaining salmon, chives. Serve warm.

Nutrition (per Serving): Calories 243 Carbs 2g Fat 18 g Protein 14g

CHAPTER 6: PORK AND LAMB

Pork and Zucchini Lasagna

Prep Time: 15 minutes | Cooking Time: 8 hours

Ingredients (4 Servings):

- 2 cup minced lean ground pork
- 4 medium zucchinis
- 2 diced small onion
- 1 minced clove of garlic
- 2 cans Italian diced tomatoes
- 2 tbsp olive oil
- 2 cup shredded Mozzarella cheese
- 2 eggs
- 1 tbsp dried basil
- 2 tbsp butter

Directions:

Slice the zucchini lengthwise into 6 slices. Heat-up the olive oil in a saucepan, then sauté the garlic and onions for 5 minutes. Put the minced meat, cook for a further 5 minutes, put the tomatoes, and cook for an additional 5 minutes. Add the seasoning and mix thoroughly.

Mix the egg plus cheese in a small bowl, and whisk. Grease the slow cooker using the butter, and then begin to layer the lasagna. First, layer with the zucchini slices, add the meat mixture, then top with the cheese. Repeat and finish with the cheese—Cook for 8 hours on low.

Nutrition (per Serving): Carbs 74g Protein 39g Fat 38g Calories 808

Delicious BBQ Ribs

Prep Time: 15 minutes | Cooking Time: 8 hours

Ingredients (4 Servings):

- 3 lb. pork ribs
- 2 tbsp olive oil
- 1 can tomato paste
- ½ cup hot water
- ½ cup vinegar
- 6 tbsp Worcestershire sauce
- 4 tbsp dry mustard
- 1 tbsp chili powder
- 1 tsp ground cumin
- 1 tsp powdered sweetener of your choice

Directions:

Heat the olive oil in a large frying pan and brown the ribs, then put in the slow cooker.

Combine the rest of the fixings in a small bowl, whisk thoroughly and pour over the ribs—Cook for 8 hours on low. Serve.

Nutrition (per Serving): Carbs 34 g Protein 35g Fat 38 g Calories 630

Coconut Pork Curry

Prep Time: 15 minutes | Cooking Time: 8 hours

Ingredients (6 Servings):

- 2 lb. cubed pork shoulder
- 2 tbsp coconut oil
- 2 tbsp olive oil
- 2 diced yellow onion
- 2 cloves minced garlic
- 3 tbsp tomato paste
- 1 can coconut milk
- 1 cup water
- ½ cup white wine
- 1 tsp turmeric
- 1 tsp ginger powder
- 1 tsp curry powder
- ½ tsp paprika

Directions:

Heat-up 1 tbsp of olive oil in a saucepan and sauté the garlic and onions for 3 minutes.

Add the pork and brown it, and then add the tomato paste. Mix the remaining ingredients in the slow cooker and then add the pork. Cook for 8 hours on low. Divide onto plates and serve.

Nutrition (per Serving): Carbs 3g Protein 31g Fat 19g Calories 322

Kalua Pork

Prep Time: 15 minutes | Cooking Time: 8 hours

Ingredients (8 Servings):

- 4 lb. pork shoulder roast
- 1 tbsp liquid smoke
- 2 tsp sea salt

Directions:

Place pork roast into the slow cooker. Pour liquid smoke and sea salt all over the pork roast.

Cook within 8 hours, low. Shred the meat, then serve.

Nutrition (per Serving): Calories 582 Fat 46.2 g Carbs 0 g Protein 38.1 g

Tasty Coconut Pork

Prep Time: 15 minutes | Cooking Time: 8 hours

Ingredients (6 Servings):

- 3 lb. pork shoulder, boneless and cut into chunks
- ½ cup fresh cilantro, chopped
- 1 cup coconut water
- 1/4 cup fish sauce
- 3 tbsp olive oil
- 4 scallions, chopped

Directions:

Heat-up olive oil in a pan over medium heat. Brown the meat in hot oil. Transfer meat into the slow cooker. Add the rest of the items into the slow cooker and mix well. Cook on low within 8 hours. Serve and enjoy.

Nutrition (per Serving): Calories 354 Fat 27.3 g Carbs 3.6 g Protein 47 g

Adobo Pulled Pork

Prep Time: 15 minutes | Cooking Time: 8 hours

Ingredients (4 Servings):

- 2 lb. pork
- 1 tbsp ground cumin
- 1 tbsp garlic, minced
- 7 oz chipotle peppers in adobo sauce
- 1 can chicken broth

Directions:

Put all listed items into the slow cooker and stir well. Cook within 8 hours on low.

Shred the meat using a fork. Stir well and serve.

Nutrition (per Serving): Calories 391 Fat 9.9 g Carbs 10.1 g Sugar 3 g Protein 62 g

Delicious Pork Tacos

Prep Time: 15 minutes | Cooking Time: 8 hours

Ingredients (8 Servings):

- 2 lb. pork tenderloin
- 2 tsp cayenne pepper
- 20 oz salsa
- 3 tsp garlic powder
- 2 tbsp ground cumin
- 2 tbsp chili powder

Directions:

Place pork tenderloin into the slow cooker. Mix all rest of the ingredients except salsa in a small bowl. Rub spice mixture over pork tenderloin. Pour salsa on top of pork tenderloin.

Cook within 8 hours, low. Transfer the pork from slow cooker, and shred using a fork.

Return shredded pork into the slow cooker and stir well with salsa. Serve and enjoy.

Nutrition (per Serving): Calories 202 Fat 4.9 g Carbs 8 g Protein 31.7 g

Onion Pork Chops

Prep Time: 15 minutes | Cooking Time: 6 hours

Ingredients (6 Servings):

- 2 lb. pork chops, boneless
- ½ tsp garlic powder
- 1 tbsp apple cider vinegar
- 2 tbsp Worcestershire sauce
- 1/3 cup butter, sliced
- 1 large onion, sliced
- A pinch of red pepper flakes
- 1 tbsp olive oil

Directions:

Heat-up the olive oil in a pan over medium-high heat. Brown pork chops in hot oil from both sides. Add remaining ingredients except for onion and butter into the slow cooker and stir well. Place brown pork chops into the slow cooker and top with butter and onion. Cook within 6 hours, low. Serve and enjoy.

Nutrition (per Serving): Calories 309 Fat 19.2 g Carbs 3.5 g Protein 34.4 g

Creamy Pork Chops

Prep Time: 15 minutes | Cooking Time: 4 hours

Ingredients (4 Servings):

- 4 pork chops, boneless
- 1 cup chicken or vegetable stock
- ½ cup sour cream
- 1 can onion soup

Directions:

Pour chicken broth into the slow cooker. Place pork chops into the slow cooker.

Cook within 3 1/2 hours, low. Once it is done, then open the slow cooker and drain juices from the slow cooker. Mix the sour cream plus onion soup in a small bowl and pour over pork chops. Cook again within 30 minutes, low. Serve and enjoy.

Nutrition (per Serving): Calories 411 Fat 27.1 g Carbs 17.4 g Protein 30.3 g

Bay Leaf Pork Roast Shoulder

Prep Time: 15 minutes | Cooking Time: 8 hours

Ingredients (4 Servings):

- 3 lb. of whole pork shoulder
- 1 can Italian diced tomatoes
- 1 diced sweet onion
- 2 chopped cloves of garlic
- 4 tbsp lard
- 1 cup of water
- 1 bay leaf
- ¼ tsp of ground cloves

Directions:

Put all the items in the slow cooker. Cook for 8 hours on low. Serve.

Nutrition (per Serving): Carbs 5 g Protein 69 g Fat 30 g Calories 577

Dressed Pork Leg Roast

Prep Time: 15 minutes | Cooking Time: 8 hours

Ingredients (12 Servings):

- 8 lb. pork leg
- 2 tbsp butter
- 1 yellow onion, sliced
- 4 garlic cloves, peeled and minced
- 2 tbsp ground cumin
- 2 tbsp ground thyme
- 2 tbsp ground chili
- 1 cup hot water

Directions:

Butter the slow cooker. Slice crisscrosses along the top of the pork leg. Arrange onion slices and minced garlic along the bottom of the slow cooker. Place meat on top of vegetables. In a small bowl, mix the herbs. Rub it all over the pork leg. Add the water. Cover, cook on high for 8 hours. Remove and transfer, cover with foil. Let it rest for 1 hour. Shred the meat and serve.

Nutrition (per Serving): Calories 428 Carbs 0g Fat 17g Protein 62g

Lamb Roast

Prep Time: 15 minutes | Cooking Time: 8 hours

Ingredients (8 Servings):

- 1 lamb joint (approximately 4.5 lb.) at room temperature

- 10 medium radishes, scrubbed, washed, and cut in half
- 1 red onion, diced
- 2 garlic cloves, minced
- 2 tbsp olive oil
- 1 tsp dry oregano
- 1 tsp dry thyme
- 1 sprig fresh rosemary
- 4 cups broth, your choice

Directions:

Place cut radishes along the bottom of the slow cooker. Season. Add onion and garlic.

Blend the herbs plus olive oil in a small bowl until it forms to paste. Place the meat on top of the radishes. Knead the paste over the meat. Heat the stock, pour it around the meat. Cover, cook on low for 8 hours. Let it rest for 20 minutes. Slice and serve.

Nutrition (per Serving): Calories 348 Carbs 4g Fat 14g Protein 47g

Kashmiri Lamb Curry

Prep Time: 40 minutes | Cooking Time: 7 hours

Ingredients (6 Servings):

- 2 lb. lamb meat
- 3 tomatoes, chopped
- ¼ cup unsweetened coconut meat, shredded
- 3 long green fresh chili peppers
- 4 dried red chili peppers
- 1 tsp garam masala
- 1 tsp cumin seeds
- 4 cloves of garlic, crushed
- 1-piece ginger root, peeled and grated
- 2 large onions, sliced
- 6 tbsp vegetable oil

- ½ ground turmeric
- 1 cup plain yogurt
- ¼ cup cilantro, chopped
- 1 cup water

Directions:

Take the chilies, garam masala, cumin seeds, garlic, ginger, tomatoes, and coconut in a blender and pulse until smooth. Set aside. In a skillet, heat vegetable oil and sauté the onions and lamb meat for 3 minutes. Transfer the meat mixture to the slow cooker. Pour in chili paste mixture on top of the lamb. Add the turmeric, yogurt, cilantro, and water—season with pepper and salt. Cook within 7 hours, low, until tender.

Nutrition (per Serving): Calories 350 Carbs 3g Protein 25g Fat 25g

Tasty Lamb Shoulders

Prep Time: 15 minutes | Cooking Time: 4 hours

Ingredients (4 Servings):

- 2 lb. lamb shoulder
- 1/4 cup beef or chicken broth
- 1/4 cup fresh mint
- 1/4 cup onion, chopped
- 1/4 lb. carrots
- 2 tbsp spice rub

Directions:

Pour beef broth into the slow cooker. Rub spice on all over the lamb shoulder and place lamb shoulder into the slow cooker. Add remaining ingredients into the slow cooker—Cook within 4 hours on high. Shred the meat using a fork. Serve and enjoy.

Nutrition (per Serving): Calories 320 Fat 16.8 g Carbs 4 g Protein 45 g

Thyme Lamb Chops

Prep Time: 15 minutes | Cooking Time: 6 hours

Ingredients (2 Servings):

- 2 lamb shoulder chops, bone-in
- ¼ cup fresh thyme
- 1 tsp garlic paste
- ½ cup red wine
- 1 cup beef or vegetable broth

Directions:

Put all fixings into the slow cooker and mix well. Cook within 6 hours, low setting. Serve and enjoy.

Nutrition (per Serving): Calories 322 Fat 20g Carbs 2.4 g Protein 25.1g

Garlic and Herbs Lamb Chops

Prep Time: 15 minutes | Cooking Time: 4 hours

Ingredients (4 Servings):

- 8 lamb loin chops
- 2 garlic cloves, minced
- ½ tsp garlic powder
- ½ tsp dried thyme
- 2 tsp dried oregano
- 1 medium onion, sliced

Directions:

Mix oregano, garlic powder, thyme, pepper, and salt in a small bowl. Rub herb mixture over the lamb chops. Place lamb chops into the slow cooker—top lamb chops with garlic and sliced onion. Cook within 4 hours, low. Serve and enjoy.

Nutrition (per Serving): Calories 550 Fat 40g Carbs 3 g Protein 44.5 g

Barbacoa Lamb

Prep Time: 25 minutes | Cooking Time: 6 hours

Ingredients (12 Servings):

- 6 lb. leg of lamb - boneless
- ¼ cup dried mustard

  2 tbsp of each:
- smoked paprika
- himalayan salt

  1 tbsp of each:
- chipotle powder
- dried oregano
- ground cumin
- 1 cup water

Directions:

Combine the paprika, oregano, chipotle powder, cumin, and salt.

Cover the roast with the dried mustard, and sprinkle with the prepared spices. Arrange the lamb in the slow cooker, cover, and let it marinate in the refrigerator overnight.

In the morning, let the pot come to room temperature. Once you're ready to cook, just add the water to the slow cooker on the high heat setting—Cook for 6 hours.

When done, remove all except for one cup of the cooking juices, and shred the lamb.

Using the rest of the cooking juices, adjust the seasoning as you desire, and serve.

Nutrition (per Serving): Calories 510 Carbs 1.2 g Fat 35.8 g Protein 57.5 g

Lamb Provençal

Prep Time: 15 minutes | Cooking Time: 8 hours

Ingredients (4 Servings):

- 2 racks lamb, approximately 2 lb.
- 2 tbsp olive oil
- 2 tbsp fresh rosemary, chopped
- 1 tbsp fresh thyme, chopped
- 4 garlic cloves, minced

- 1 tsp dry oregano
- 1 lemon, the zest
- 1 tsp minced fresh ginger
- 1 cup red wine, good quality

Directions:

Preheat the slow cooker on low. In a pan, heat 1 tbsp olive oil. Brown the meat for 2 minutes per side. Mix remaining ingredients in a bowl. Place the lamb in the slow cooker, pour the remaining seasoning over the meat. Cover, cook on low for 8 hours.

Nutrition (per Serving): Calories 390 Carbs 3g Fat 19g Protein 41g

Greek Style Lamb Shanks

Prep Time: 15 minutes | Cooking Time: 6 hours

Ingredients (8 Servings):

- 4 lamb shanks, approx.. 1 lb. each
- 4 tbsp butter
- 2 tbsp olive oil
- 8-10 small onions
- 4 garlic cloves, minced
- 2 beef tomatoes, cubed
- ¼ cup of green olives
- 4 bay leaves
- 1 sprig fresh rosemary
- 1 tsp dry thyme
- 1 tsp ground cumin
- 1 cup fresh spinach
- ¾ cup hot water
- ½ cup red wine

Directions:

Liquify the butter in a pan, then cook the shanks on each side. Remove, then add oil, onions, garlic Cook for 3-4 minutes. Add tomatoes, olives, spices, then stir well. Put the liquids and return the meat. Boil for 1 minute. Transfer

everything to the slow cooker. Cover, cook on medium-high for 6 hours.

Nutrition (per Serving): Calories 398 Carbs 3g Fat 16g Protein 22g

Minty Lamb with Green Beans

Prep Time: 15 minutes | Cooking Time: 10 hours

Ingredients (4 Servings):

- 1 lamb leg – bone-in
- 6 cup trimmed green beans
- 2 tbsp lard/ghee/tallow
- 4 garlic cloves
- ¼ freshly chopped mint/1-2 tbsp dried mint

Directions:

Heat-up the slow cooker with a high setting. Dry the lamb with some paper towels. Sprinkle with the pepper and salt. Grease a Dutch oven or similar large pot with the ghee/lard.

Sear the lamb until golden brown and set aside. Remove the peels from the garlic and mince—dice up the mint. Arrange the seared meat into the slow cooker and give it a shake of the garlic and mint. Secure the lid and program the cooker on the low-heat function (10 hrs.) or the high-function (6 hrs.). After about four hours, switch the lamb out of the cooker. Toss in the green beans and return the lamb into the pot. Let the flavors mingle for about two more hours. The meat should be tender and the beans crispy. Serve.

Nutrition (per Serving): Calories 525 Carbs 7.6 g Protein 37.3 g Fat 36.4 g

Balsamic Lamb Chops

Prep Time: 15 minutes | Cooking Time: 6 hours

Ingredients (6 Servings):

- 3 lb. lamb chops, trimmed off
- 2 tbsp rosemary
- 3 tbsp balsamic vinegar
- 4 garlic cloves, minced
- 1 large onion, sliced

Directions:

Put the onion to the bottom of the slow cooker. Place lamb chops on top of onions, add rosemary, vinegar, garlic, pepper, and salt. Cook within 6 hours on low. Serve and enjoy.

Nutrition (per Serving): Calories 305 Fat 15.1 g Carbs 3.9 g Protein 40g

Succulent Lamb

Prep Time: 20 minutes | Cooking Time: 8 hours

Ingredients (6 Servings):

- 1 (2 lb.) leg of lamb
- ¼ cup olive oil
- 1 tbsp maple syrup
- 2 tbsp whole grain mustard
- 4 thyme sprigs
- 6-7 mint leaves
- 1 tsp dried rosemary
- 1 tsp garlic powder

Directions:

Cut the string off of the lamb, then slice three slits over the top. Cover the meat with the oil and the rub (mustard, pepper, salt, and maple syrup). Put the rosemary plus garlic into the slits. Prepare on the low setting for 7 hours. Garnish with the mint and thyme—Cook 1 more hour. Place on a platter and serve.

Nutrition (per Serving): Calories 340 Carbs 0.3 g Fat 37.2 g Protein 76.7 g

Tarragon Lamb & Beans

Prep Time: 15 minutes | Cooking Time: 9 hours

Ingredients (6 Servings):

- 4 (1 ½ lb.) lamb shanks
- 1 can white beans/cannellini
- 1 cup peeled - diced carrot
- 2 sliced garlic cloves
- 1 cup onion
- ¾ cup celery
- 2 tsp dried tarragon
- ¼ tsp freshly cracked black pepper
- 2 tsp dried tarragon
- 1 can (28 oz) diced tomatoes - not drained

Recommended: 7-quart slow cooker

Directions:

Discard all the fat from the lamb shanks. Pour the beans, cloves of garlic, chopped carrots, chopped celery, and onion in the cooker. Put the shanks over the beans, and sprinkle with the salt, pepper, and tarragon. Empty the tomatoes over the lamb - including the juices— Cook, the lamb in the slow cooker on high for approximately one hour.

Reduce the temperature to the low setting and cook for eight hours or until the lamb is tender. Remove, and set it aside. Empty the bean mixture through a colander over a bowl to reserve the liquid. Let the juices stand for five minutes and skim off the fat from the surface.

Return the bean mixture to the liquid in the slow cooker. Strip the lamb bones and throw the bones away. Serve with the bean mixture and enjoy.

Nutrition (per Serving): Calories 353 Carbs 32.9 g Fat 6.3 g Protein 24.3 g

Apricot Pulled Pork

Prep Time: 15 minutes | Cooking Time: 11 hours

Ingredients (6 Servings):

- 2 lb. pork
- 1 cup barbecue sauce
- 6 oz dried apricots
- 4 lb. apricot spread that does not contain any sugar
- 1 sweet onion, sliced

Directions:

Put the pork in the cooker. Add the barbecue, apricots, spread, and onions. Low cook for 11 hours. Serve.

Nutrition (per Serving): Calories 715 Fat 8g Protein 33 g Carbs 120 g

Pork Chops with Cumin Butter

Prep Time: 15 minutes | Cooking Time: 4 hours

Ingredients (6 Servings):

- 2 lb. pork sirloin chops with the bone
- ½ cup salsa
- 4 tbsp butter
- 4 tbsp lime juice
- 1 tsp ground cumin
- ¾ tsp garlic powder

Directions:

Combine the spices and season the pork chops. Melt the butter in a saucepan and brown the pork chops for 3 minutes on each side. Put it inside the slow cooker and pour the salsa over the top. Cook on high within 3-4 hours. Divide onto plates and serve.

Nutrition (per Serving): Calories 562 Fat 40 g Carbs 6g Protein 33g

Mexican Carne Adovada

Prep Time: 30 minutes | Cooking Time: 6 hours

Ingredients (4 Servings):

- 2 lb. pork shoulder, cubes
- 2 tsp apple cider vinegar
- 1 tsp ground cumin
- 2 tsp dried Mexican oregano
- 4 garlic, sliced
- 1 onion, sliced
- 2 cups chicken stock
- 6 oz dried chilies, rinsed

Directions:

Put all the items in a pot, except the pork. Simmer it within 30-60 minutes, low.

Remove, then cooldown it within a few minutes. Puree the batter in batches using a blender.

Put now the pork meat in a baking dish, covering it with the sauce. Chill within 1 to 2 days to marinate, stirring frequently. Cook it in a slow cooker within 4 to 6 hours, low. Serve warm.

Nutrition (per Serving): Calories 320.2 Fat 12.3g Carb 2.3g Protein 48g

Smoky Pork with Cabbage

Prep Time: 10 minutes | Cooking Time: 8 hours

Ingredients (6 Servings):

- 2 lb. pastured pork roast
- 1/3 cup liquid smoke
- ½ cabbage head, chopped
- 1 cup water

Directions:

Rub pork with salt and place into the slow cooker. Pour liquid smoke over the pork. Add water. Cover slow cooker with lid and cook on low for 7 hours. Remove pork from slow cooker and add cabbage in the bottom of slow cooker. Now place pork on top of the cabbage.

Cover again and cook for 1 hour more. Shred pork with a fork and serve.

Nutrition (per Serving): Calories 223 Fat 8g Carbs 4g Protein 35.4g

Simple Roasted Pork Shoulder

Prep Time: 10 minutes | Cooking Time: 9 hours

Ingredients (6 Servings):

- 2 ½ lb. pork shoulder
- 1 tsp garlic powder
- ½ cup water

Directions:

Season pork with garlic powder, pepper, and salt and place in slow cooker. Add water.

Cover slow cooker with lid and cook on high for 1 hour then turn heat to low and cook for 8 hours. Remove meat from slow cooker and shred using a fork. Serve.

Nutrition (per Serving): Calories 497 Fat 40g Carbs 0.3 g Protein 33g

Flavors Pork Chops

Prep Time: 10 minutes | Cooking Time: 4 hours

Ingredients (4 Servings):

- 8 pork chops
- 2 garlic cloves, minced
- 1 cup chicken broth
- 1 tbsp poultry seasoning
- ¼ cup olive oil

Directions:

In a bowl, whisk together olive oil, poultry seasoning, garlic, broth, pepper, and salt.

Pour olive oil mixture into the slow cooker then place pork chops into the slow cooker. Cover slow cooker with lid and cook on high for 4 hours. Serve.

Nutrition (per Serving): Calories 386 Fat 22g Carbs 2.9 g Protein 49g

Pork Loin with Peanut Sauce

Prep Time: 10 minutes | Cooking Time: 8 hours

Ingredients (8 Servings):

- 2 lb. pork tenderloin
- 3 tbsp olive oil
- 2 cup cabbage, shredded
- 1 ½ cup chicken stock
- ½ cup peanut butter
- ¼ cup soy sauce
- 1 tbsp rice vinegar
- 1 tbsp crushed red pepper flakes
- 1 tbsp cayenne pepper sauce
- 2 cloves garlic crushed and minced
- ½ cup peanuts, chopped
- 1 tbsp fresh lemongrass, chopped

Directions:

Brush the tenderloin with olive oil and season it with salt and black pepper.

Arrange the tenderloin and cabbage in a slow cooker. In a bowl, combine the chicken stock, peanut butter, soy sauce, rice vinegar, crushed red pepper flakes, cayenne pepper sauce, and garlic. Whisk them together and pour the sauce into the slow cooker. Stir gently to distribute the sauce. Sprinkle in the peanuts and lemongrass. Cover and cook on low for 8 hours.

Nutrition (per Serving): Calories 376, Fat 25.5 g, Carbs 6.9 g, Protein 29g

Creamy Herbed Tenderloin

Prep Time: 10 minutes | Cooking Time: 6 hours

Ingredients (6 Servings):

- 2 lb. pork tenderloin
- 1 cup chicken stock
- 2 tbsp olive oil
- 2 cloves garlic, crushed and minced
- 1 tbsp fresh oregano
- ½ cup fresh parsley, chopped
- 3 cups broccoli florets
- 1 cup onion, sliced
- 2 cups heavy cream, warmed

Directions:

Heat the olive oil in a skillet over medium-high heat. Season the tenderloin with salt and black pepper. Place the tenderloin in the skillet and brown it on all sides, approximately 5 minutes. Remove the tenderloin from the heat and season it with the garlic, oregano, and parsley, using your hands to pat it into the surface of the meat as necessary.

Place the tenderloin in the slow cooker, along with the broccoli and onion. Combine the heavy cream and chicken stock. Pour the liquid into the slow cooker. Cover and cook on low for 6 hours, or until the cream has thickened and the pork has cooked through.

Nutrition (per Serving): Calories 314.4, Fat 17.1 g, Carbs 5.8 g, Protein 36.2 g

Traditional Sausages and Peppers

Prep Time: 10 minutes | Cooking Time: 6 hours

Ingredients (6 Servings):

- 2 lb. spicy Italian sausage links
- ¼ cup olive oil
- ½ cup dry red wine
- 3 cloves garlic, crushed and minced
- 2 cups green bell peppers, sliced thick
- 1 cup red bell peppers, sliced thick
- 1 cup onion, sliced thick
- 1 tbsp fresh thyme, chopped
- ½ cup fresh grated Parmesan cheese

Directions:

Heat the olive oil in a skillet over medium-high heat. Add the sausage links to the skillet and cook until browned on all sides, approximately 5-7 minutes. Add the red wine to the skillet and cook for 2-3 minutes, until the wine reduces, taking the time to scrape any browned bits off the bottom of the skillet. Remove the skillet from the heat. Add the green bell pepper, red bell pepper, onion, garlic, salt, black pepper, and thyme to the slow cooker. Toss to mix. Add the sausages and any pan sauce. Cover the slow cooker and cook on low for 6 hours. Sprinkle with freshly grated Parmesan cheese before serving.

Nutrition (per Serving): Calories 509, Fat 35g, Carbs 12.5 g, Protein 31.3 g

Pork Ribs

Prep Time: 10 minutes | Cooking Time: 8 hours

Ingredients (6 Servings):

- 2 lb. pork spareribs
- ¼ cup apple cider vinegar
- ¼ cup Worcestershire sauce
- 3 tbsp tomato paste
- 1 tsp dark molasses
- 1 tbsp spicy mustard
- 1 tbsp prepared horseradish
- 1 tsp chili powder
- 2 cloves garlic, crushed and minced

Directions:

In a saucepan, combine the apple cider vinegar, Worcestershire sauce, tomato paste, molasses, mustard, horseradish, chili powder, and garlic. Mix well and bring the mixture to a boil over medium-high heat. Reduce the heat to low and let the sauce simmer for 15 minutes. Remove it from the heat and allow it to cool slightly. Cut the ribs into smaller sections and place them in the slow cooker. Pour the sauce over the ribs and toss to make sure the sauce coats the ribs evenly on all sides. Cover and cook for 8 hours on low.

Preheat the broiler and line a baking sheet with aluminum foil. Remove the ribs from the slow cooker and place them on the baking sheet. Place them under the broiler for 3-5 minutes before serving.

Nutrition (per Serving): Calories 594.8, Fat 41.9 g, Carbs 2.6 g Protein 43g

Salsa Pork Chops

Prep Time: 10 minutes | Cooking Time: 3 hours

Ingredients (8 Servings):

- 8 pork chops, bone-in
- 4 tbsp olive oil
- 1 tsp garlic powder
- ½ tsp ground cumin
- ¼ cup fresh lime juice
- ½ cup salsa

Directions:

Add all ingredients into the cooking pot and stir well. Cover and cook on HIGH for 3 hours. Serve.

Nutrition (per Serving): Calories 255 Fat 15 g Carbs 4.5 g Protein 24g

Curried Pork Chops

Prep Time: 10 minutes | Cooking Time: 6 hours

Ingredients (6 Servings):

- 2 lb. pork chops
- 1 tbsp dried rosemary
- 1/4 cup olive oil
- 1 tbsp ground cumin
- 1 tbsp fennel seeds
- 2 tbsp fresh chives, chopped
- 1 tbsp curry powder
- 1 tbsp dried thyme

Directions:

In a small bowl, mix cumin, rosemary, 2 tbsp oil, fennel seeds, chives, curry powder, thyme, and salt. Rub cumin mixture over pork chops. Place pork chops into the cooking pot.

Pour remaining olive oil over pork chops. Cover and cook on LOW for 6 hours. Serve.

Nutrition (per Serving): Calories 227 Fat 11g Carbs 5.1 g Protein 29.8 g

Poultry Seasoned Pork Chops

Prep Time: 10 minutes | Cooking Time: 4 hours

Ingredients (4 Servings):

- 4 pork chops
- 2 tbsp garlic powder
- 2 garlic cloves, minced
- 1 cup chicken broth
- 1 tsp dried basil
- 1 tsp dried oregano
- 2 tbsp poultry seasoning
- ¼ cup olive oil

Directions:

In a large bowl, whisk together oil, basil, oregano, poultry seasoning, garlic powder, garlic, and broth. Pour bowl mixture into the cooking pot then place pork chops into the cooking pot. Cover and cook on HIGH for 4 hours. Serve and enjoy.

Nutrition (per Serving): Calories 247 Fat 15g Carbs 3.1 g Protein 24.8 g

No Stick Ribs

Prep Time: 10 minutes | Cooking Time: 8 hours

Ingredients (6 Servings):

- 2 lb. pork ribs
- ¼ cup olive oil
- 1 tsp chili powder
- 2 tsp coriander
- 1 cup chicken stock

Directions:

Brush the ribs with olive oil and season them with salt, black pepper, chili powder, and coriander. Cut the ribs into smaller sections, if desired, and place them in the slow cooker.

Add the chicken stock. Cover and cook on low for 8 hours. Serve.

Nutrition (per Serving): Calories 632 Fat 45 g Carbs 1.1 g Protein 43.8 g

Macadamia Crusted Pork Steaks

Prep Time: 10 minutes | Cooking Time: 6 hours

Ingredients (4 Servings):

- 1 lb. boneless pork steaks
- 1 tsp allspice
- ½ tsp nutmeg
- ½ tsp ground ginger
- ½ tsp thyme
- ¼ cup buttermilk
- ½ cup macadamia nuts, chopped
- ¼ cup unsweetened shredded coconut
- 2 tbsp coconut oil
- 1 tbsp jalapeño pepper, diced
- ½ cup chicken stock
- 2 tbsp lime juice
- 4 cups fresh spinach

Directions:

In a bowl, combine allspice, nutmeg, ginger, thyme, and buttermilk. Whisk together well. Place the pork chops in the bowl and cover them with the buttermilk mixture. Allow them to saturate for 15 minutes. In another bowl, combine the macadamia nuts and coconut. Remove each pork chop and coat it on both sides with the crushed macadamia nuts and coconut. Heat the coconut oil in a skillet over medium heat.

Add the pork chops and brown for approximately 2 minutes per side. Place the spinach, jalapeño pepper, chicken stock, and lime juice in the slow cooker and stir gently to mix.

Add the pork steaks, cover, and cook on low for 5 ½ hours. Serve.

Nutrition (per Serving): Calories 181.6, Fat 11.4 g Carbs 5.8 g, Protein 24.5 g

Feta Meatballs

Prep Time: 10 minutes | Cooking Time: 6 hours

Ingredients (8 Servings):

- 1 lb. ground pork
- 1 lb. ground beef
- 1 cup summer squash, shredded
- ½ cup celery, diced
- ½ cup onion, diced
- 1 cup feta cheese
- 2 eggs
- 1 tsp oregano
- 1 tsp thyme
- 1 tsp garlic powder
- 3 tbsp olive oil
- 1 cup chicken stock
- 1 cup tomatoes, chopped
- 1 tbsp capers
- ¼ cup fresh basil

Directions:

In a large bowl, combine the ground pork, ground beef, summer squash, celery, onion, feta cheese, and eggs. Mix well. Season the mixture with salt, black pepper, oregano, thyme, and garlic powder. Once the mixture has been seasoned, take large spoonful of it and form them into golf ball sized meatballs. Heat the olive oil in a skillet over medium heat.

Add the meatballs to the skillet and brown on all sides for approximately 5 minutes. Transfer the meatballs from the skillet into a slow cooker. In a blender, combine the chicken stock, tomatoes, capers, and basil. Blend until smooth and then pour the sauce into the slow cooker. Cover and cook on low for 6 hours. Serve.

Nutrition (per Serving): Calories 222 Fat 13.7 g Carbs 3.6 g Protein 24.9g

Lamb and Asparagus

Prep Time: 10 minutes | Cooking Time: 6 hours

Ingredients (6 Servings):

- 2 lb. lamb stew meat
- ¼ cup butter, melted
- 2 tsp marjoram
- 1 tsp caraway seed, ground
- 2 cloves garlic, crushed and minced
- 1 ½ cup onion, chopped
- 4 cups asparagus spears, cut
- 1 cup chicken stock
- 1 cup lemon slices

Directions:

Pour the melted butter into a slow cooker. Season the meat with salt, black pepper, marjoram, and caraway seed. Add the stew meat to the slow cooker, along with the garlic, onion, and asparagus, and mix together. Pour the chicken stock into the slow cooker and cover the contents with lemon slices. Cover and cook on low for 6 hours.

Nutrition (per Serving): Calories 276.5 Fat 16g Carbs 1.4g Protein 26g

Italian Style Lamb with Brussels Sprouts

Prep Time: 10 minutes | Cooking Time: 8 hours

Ingredients (6 Servings):

- 2 lb. lamb stew meat
- ¼ cup olive oil
- 1 cup onion, sliced
- 2 cups Brussels sprouts, halved
- 2 cups tomatoes, chopped
- 2 cloves garlic, crushed and minced
- ¼ cup fresh basil, chopped
- ¼ cup fresh parsley, chopped
- 2 tsp fresh thyme
- ½ cup water
- ¼ cup butter, cubed

Directions:

Season the lamb meat with salt and black pepper.

Heat the olive oil in a skillet over medium heat. Add the lamb to the skillet and cook until browned. Place the onions and Brussels sprouts in the slow cooker, followed by the lamb.

In a bowl, combine the tomatoes with the garlic, basil, parsley, and thyme. Toss to mix.

Add the tomato mixture to the slow cooker. Pour in the water and top the contents with cubed butter. Cover and cook on low for 8 hours. Serve.

Nutrition (per Serving): Calories 311 Fat 23.0g Carbs 2.7g Protein 26g

Asian Lamb

Prep Time: 10 minutes | Cooking Time: 4 hours

Ingredients (6 Servings):

- 3 lb. lamb shoulder
- ¼ cup rice wine vinegar
- 1 tbsp garlic, minced
- 2 tbsp olive oil
- ¼ cup brown sugar
- ¼ cup hoisin sauce
- ½ cup soy sauce

Directions:

Add oil into the cooking pot. Put lamb shoulder into the cooking pot and sauté until brown from all the sides. Mix remaining ingredients and pour over meat. Cover and cook on HIGH for 2 hours. Turn lamb, cover, and cook on HIGH for 2 hours more. Serve.

Nutrition (per Serving): Calories 308 Fat 15.3g Carbs 2g Protein 41g

Moroccan Lamb

Prep Time: 10 minutes | Cooking Time: 4 hours

Ingredients (6 Servings):

- 2 lb. lamb chops
- 1 cup beef or chicken stock
- ½ cup dried apricots, chopped
- 1 cup yogurt
- 2 tbsp flour
- 10 oz can tomato, crushed
- 10 oz can chickpeas, rinsed & drained
- 1 carrot, chopped
- 1 onion, sliced
- 1 tsp turmeric
- 1 tsp ground ginger
- 1 tsp ground coriander
- 1 tsp ground cumin

Directions:

In a bowl, mix together stock and spices. Add lamb chops and remaining ingredients into the cooking pot. Pour stock mixture over lamb chops. Cover with lid and cook on High for 4 hours. Serve and enjoy.

Nutrition (per Serving): Calories 340 Fat 13g Carbs 25 g Protein 27.5g

Moroccan Lamb Stew

Prep Time: 10 minutes | Cooking Time: 8 hours

Ingredients (6 Servings):

- 2 lb. lamb shoulder, cut into chunks
- 2 tsp thyme
- ½ cup beef or chicken stock
- 14 oz can tomato, chopped
- 2 tbsp honey
- 2 garlic cloves, minced
- 1 onion, sliced
- 2 tbsp olive oil

Directions:

Add all ingredients into the cooking pot and stir well. Cover and cook on Low for 8 hours. Stir well and serve.

Nutrition (per Serving): Calories 348 Fat 13g Carbs 23g Protein 27g

S A L T & P E P P E R *the list of ingredient list do not indicate the amount of salt and pepper: you can add approximately a teaspoon of salt and, in if you like it, 1/2 teaspoon of pepper for each recipe*

CHAPTER 7: BEEF

Slow cooker Beef Roast

Prep Time: 20 minutes | Cooking Time: 8 hours

Ingredients (6 Servings):

- 2 lb. beef chuck roast, trimmed of excess fat
- 2 tbsp fresh basil, chopped
- 3 cloves of garlic, minced
- 2 bay leaves
- 1 large yellow onion, chopped
- 2 cup beef or chicken stock

Directions:

Pat dries the beef with a paper towel and rub with salt, pepper, and chopped basil. Take inside the slow cooker and spread the onion, garlic, and bay leaves. Pour over the beef stock, then cook on low within 8 hours until tender. Serve.

Nutrition (per Serving): Calories 234 Carbs 2g Fat 16g Protein 21g

Beef and Cabbage Roast

Prep Time: 15 minutes | Cooking Time: 8 hours

Ingredients (10 Servings):

- 4 lb. beef brisket (two pieces)
- 1 red onion, quartered
- 2 garlic cloves, minced
- 2 stocks celery, diced
- 4-6 dry pimento berries
- 2 bay leaves
- 1 tsp chili powder
- 1 tsp ground cumin
- 2 cups broth, beef
- 2 cups hot water
- 1 medium cabbage, quartered

Directions:

Add all ingredients, except cabbage, to the slow cooker in order of the list.

Cover, cook on low for 7 hours. Uncover, add the cabbage on top of the stew. Re-cover, cook for 1 additional hour. Serve.

Nutrition (per Serving): Calories 278 Carbs 4g Fat 19g Protein 25g

Coffee- Braised Brisket

Prep Time: 15 minutes | Cooking Time: 10 hours

Ingredients (6 Servings):

- 3 lb. boneless beef brisket
- 1 tbsp balsamic vinegar
- 4 cups strong brewed coffee
- 1 sliced onion
- 1 tsp garlic powder
- ½ tbsp paprika
- ½ tbsp ground cfee
- 1 tbsp coconut sugar

Directions:

Mix paprika, garlic powder, pepper, salt, and ground coffee. Remove the fat from brisket, put the batter all over its surface. Put the meat in the Slow cooker, then the onions. Mix in the vinegar plus coffee, then pour inside. Cover and now cook on low heat for 10 hours or on high heat setting for 5 hours. Serve the onion mixture with the meat.

Nutrition (per Serving): Calories 349 Proteins 32g Carbs 8g Fat 24g

Beef Shoulder with BBQ Sauce

Prep Time: 15 minutes | Cooking Time: 10 hours

Ingredients (6 Servings):

- 3 lb. beef shoulder, whole
- 2 tbsp butter
- 1 onion, diced
- 1 garlic bulb, peeled and minced
- 4 tbsp red wine vinegar
- 2 tbsp Worcestershire sauce
- 4 tbsp Swerve (or a suitable substitute)
- 1 tbsp mustard

Directions:

In a bowl, mix seasoning. Set aside. Liquify the butter in a pan, add the meat. Brown on all sides. Transfer to slow cooker. Fry the onion within 2-3 minutes in the same pan, then pour over the meat. Pour in the seasoning. Cover, cook on low for 10 hours. Remove, cover it with foil, then let it rest for 1 hour. Turn the slow cooker on high, reduce the remaining liquid by half and serve with the shredded beef.

Nutrition (per Serving): Calories 390 Carbs 5g Fat 27g Protein 32g

Meatballs and Spaghetti Squash

Prep Time: 15 minutes | Cooking Time: 8 hours

Ingredients (8 Servings):

- 1 spaghetti squash, washed, halved
- 1 tbsp butter, to grease the slow cooker
- 2 lb. lean ground beef
- 2 garlic cloves
- 1 red onion, chopped
- ½ cup almond flour
- 2 tbsp of Parmesan cheese
- 1 egg, beaten
- 1 tsp ground cumin
- 4 cans diced tomatoes
- 1 can tomato paste
- 1 cup hot water
- 1 red onion, chopped
- ¼ cup chopped parsley
- 1 bay leaf

Directions:

Grease the slow cooker, place both squash halves open side down in the slow cooker.

Mix meatball ingredients in a bowl and form approximately 20 small meatballs.

In a pan, heat the olive oil. Fry the meatballs within 2-3 minutes per side. Transfer to the slow cooker. In the small bowl, add the tomatoes, tomato paste, oil, water, onion, and parsley. Mix well. Pour the marinara sauce in the slow cooker around the squash halves. Cover, cook on low for 8 hours.

Nutrition (per Serving): Calories 235 Carbs 5g Fat 17g Protein 18.25g

Bacon and Cheeseburger Casserole

Prep Time: 20 minutes | Cooking Time: 4 hours

Ingredients (6 Servings):

- 2 lb. ground beef
- ½ onion, sliced thinly
- 1 15-oz can cream of mushroom soup
- 1 15-oz can Cheddar cheese soup
- ½ lb. bacon, cooked and crumbled
- 2 cup Cheddar cheese, grated

Directions:

Cook the ground beef plus the onions in a skillet over medium heat. Season with pepper and salt to taste. Take the beef in the slow cooker and add the cream of mushroom soup and cheese soup. Pour in the bacon and half of the cheddar cheese. Give a stir. Cook on low for 4 hours. Put the remaining cheese on top an hour before it is done cooking.

Nutrition (per Serving): Calories 589 Carbs 2 g Fat 44g Protein 45g

BBQ Beef Burritos

Prep Time: 15 minutes | Cooking Time: 8 hours

Ingredients (4 Servings):

- 2 lb. top sirloin steak

1 tsp of each:

- ground chipotle pepper – optional
- cinnamon

2 tsp of each:

- garlic powder
- 4 minced garlic cloves
- ½ white onion
- 2 bay leaves

1 cup of each:

- chicken broth
- BBQ sauce – your favorite
  Assembly Ingredients (4 Servings):
- 1 ½ cup coleslaw mix
- 8 low-carb wraps

- ½ cup mayonnaise

Directions:

Pat the steak dry using some paper towels. Slice using a sharp knife along the sides. Combine the seasonings and sprinkle on the meat. Chop the onion, then the garlic, and put to the slow cooker. Pour in the broth. Add the steak and bay leaf. Secure the lid and cook eight hours on the low setting. When done, remove the steak and drain the juices. Arrange the beef, garlic, and onion back into the cooker and shred. Put in the barbecue sauce, then stir well. Assemble the burritos using the beef fixings, a bit of slaw, and a dab of mayo.

Nutrition (per Serving): Calories 654 Carbs 20 g Fat 43 g Protein 48 g

Beef Ribs

Prep Time: 30 minutes | Cooking Time: 6 hours

Ingredients (6 Servings):

- 2 lb. beef back ribs

1 tbsp of each:

- sesame oil
- rice vinegar
- hot sauce
- garlic powder
- 1 tbsp potato starch/ cornstarch
- ¼ cup light soy sauce

Directions:

Cut and add the ribs to fit in the slow cooker. Whisk the rest of the ingredients together except for the cornstarch. Put the mixture over the ribs, making sure the sauce covers all sides. Use the low setting and cook for six hours. It will be fall off the bone tender. Prepare the oven to 200°F. Transfer the prepared ribs to a baking pan, and cover. Strain the liquid into a saucepan. Prepare on the high setting and

whisk in the cornstarch with a little bit of cold water. Continue cooking - whisking often - just until the sauce has thickened into a glaze - usually about five to ten minutes.

Brush the sauce glaze over the ribs and serve.

Nutrition (per Serving): Calories 606 Fat 45g Carbs 5g Protein 44g

Balsamic Beef

Prep Time: 15 minutes | Cooking Time: 9 hours

Ingredients (4 Servings):

- 1 lb. beef stew meat, cubed
- 1 tsp cayenne pepper
- 2 tbsp balsamic vinegar
- ½ cup of water
- 2 tbsp butter

Directions:

Toss the butter in the skillet and melt it. Then add meat and roast it for 2 minutes per side on medium heat. Transfer the meat with butter in the slow cooker. Add balsamic vinegar, cayenne pepper, and water. Close the lid and cook the meal on Low for 9 hours.

Nutrition (per Serving): Calories 166 Protein 16.5g Carbs 0.4g Fat 12.9g

Onion Beef

Prep Time: 10 minutes | Cooking Time: 5 hours

Ingredients (6 Servings):

- 3 lb. beef sirloin, sliced
- 2 cup white onion, chopped
- 1 cup of water
- ½ cup butter
- 1 bay leaf

Directions:

Mix beef sirloin with salt and ground black pepper and transfer in the slow cooker. Add butter, water, onion, and bay leaf. Close the lid and cook the meat on High for 5 hours.

Nutrition (per Serving): Calories 486, Protein 33g, Carbs 1.7g Fat 39.7g

Cilantro Beef

Prep Time: 10 minutes | Cooking Time: 4.5 hours

Ingredients (4 Servings):

- 1 lb. beef loin, roughly chopped
- ¼ cup apple cider vinegar
- 1 tbsp dried cilantro
- 1 tsp dried basil
- 1 cup of water
- 2 tsp tomato paste

Directions:

Mix meat with tomato paste, dried cilantro, and basil. Then transfer it in the slow cooker. Add apple cider vinegar and water. Cook the cilantro beef for 4.5 hours on High.

Nutrition (per Serving): Calories 181 Protein 16g Carbs 0.4g Fat 12.5g

Beef and Artichokes Bowls

Prep Time: 10 minutes | Cooking Time: 7 hours

Ingredients (2 Servings):

- 1 lb. beef sirloin, chopped
- 1 tsp cayenne pepper
- 1 tsp white pepper
- 4 artichoke hearts, chopped
- 1 cup of water

Directions:

Mix meat with white pepper and cayenne pepper. Transfer it in the slow cooker bowl. Add

salt, artichoke hearts, and water. Close the lid and cook the meal on Low for 7 hours.

Nutrition (per Serving): Calories 413 Protein 36g Carbs 6g Fat 28.9g

Mustard Beef

Prep Time: 10 minutes | Cooking Time: 8 hours

Ingredients (4 Servings):

- 1 lb. beef sirloin, chopped
- 1 tbsp capers, drained
- 1 cup of water
- 2 tbsp mustard
- 2 tbsp coconut oil

Directions:

Mix meat with mustard and leave for 10 minutes to marinate. Then melt the coconut oil in the skillet. Add meat and roast it for 1 minute per side on high heat. After this, transfer the meat in the slow cooker. Add water and capers. Cook the meal on Low for 8 hours.

Nutrition (per Serving): Calories 197 Protein 18g Carbs 2g Fat 12.1g

Beef Masala

Prep Time: 15 minutes | Cooking Time: 9 hours

Ingredients (6 Servings):

- 1 lb. beef sirloin, sliced
- 2 tsp garam masala
- 2 tbsp lemon juice
- 1 tsp ground paprika
- ½ cup coconut milk
- 2 tsp dried mint

Directions:

In the bowl mix coconut milk with dried mint, ground paprika, lemon juice, and garam masala.

Then add beef sirloin and mix the mixture. Leave it for at least 10 minutes to marinate.

Then transfer the mixture in the slow cooker. Cook it on Low for 9 hours.

Nutrition (per Serving): Calories 195 Protein 15g Carbs 2g Fat 14.5g

Beef Sautée

Prep Time: 10 minutes | Cooking Time: 8 hours

Ingredients (4 Servings):

- 1 lb. beef sirloin, chopped
- ½ cup endives, roughly chopped
- 1 tsp peppercorns - 1 carrot, diced
- 1 onion, sliced - 1 cup of water
- ½ cup tomato juice

Directions

Mix beef with onion, carrot, and peppercorns. Place the mixture in the slow cooker. Add water and tomato juice. Then close the lid and cook it on High for 5 hours. After this, add endives and cook the meal for 3 hours on Low. Serve.

Nutrition (per Serving): Calories 218 Protein 15g Carbs 6.4g Fat 12.9g

Sweet Beef

Prep Time: 10 minutes | Cooking Time: 5 hours

Ingredients (4 Servings):

- 1 lb. beef roast, sliced
- 1 tbsp maple syrup
- 2 tbsp lemon juice

- 2 tsp dried oregano
- 1 cup water

Directions:

Mix water with maple syrup, lemon juice, and dried oregano. Then pour the liquid in the slow cooker. Add beef roast and close the lid. Cook the meal on High for 5 hours.

Nutrition (per Serving): Calories 210 Protein 17g Carbs 8.4g Fat 12.9g

Thyme Beef

Prep Time: 15 minutes | Cooking Time: 5 hours

Ingredients (2 Servings):

- 1 lb. beef sirloin, chopped
- 2 tbsp dried thyme
- 2 tbsp olive oil
- ½ cup of water

Directions

Preheat the skillet well. Then mix beef with dried thyme and olive oil. Put the meat in the hot skillet and roast for 2 minutes per side on high heat. Then transfer the meat in the slow cooker. Add salt and water. Cook the meal on High for 5 hours.

Nutrition (per Serving): Calories 348 Protein 32g Carbs 2.4g Fat 24.9g

Hot Sauce Beef

Prep Time: 15 minutes | Cooking Time: 8 hours

Ingredients (4 Servings):

- 1 lb. beef sirloin, chopped
- 2 tbsp hot sauce
- 2 tbsp olive oil
- ½ cup of water

Directions

In the shallow bowl mix hot sauce with olive oil. Then mix beef sirloin with hot sauce mixture and leave for 10 minutes to marinate. Put the marinated beef in the slow cooker. Add water and close the lid. Cook the meal on Low for 8 hours.

Nutrition (per Serving): Calories 214 Protein 18g Carbs 2.4g Fat 16.9g

Beef Chops with Bean Sprouts

Prep Time: 10 minutes | Cooking Time: 7 hours

Ingredients (4 Servings):

- 1 lb. beef loin
- ½ cup bean sprouts
- 1 cup water
- 2 tbsp tomato paste
- 2 tsp chili powder

Directions:

Cut the beef loin into 5 beef chops and sprinkle them with chili powder and salt. Then place them in the slow cooker. Add water and tomato paste. Cook the meat on low for 7 hours. Then transfer the cooked beef chops in the plates, sprinkle with tomato gravy from the slow cooker, and top with bean sprouts.

Nutrition (per Serving): Calories 184 Protein 15g Carbs 2.4g Fat 12.9g

Beef Ragout with Beans

Prep Time: 10 minutes | Cooking Time: 5 hours

Ingredients (5 Servings):

- 1lb. beef stew meat, chopped
- 2 tbsp tomato paste
- 1 cup mug beans, canned
- 1 carrot, grated
- 2 cups water

Directions:

Pour water in the slow cooker. Add meat, ground black pepper, and carrot. Cook the mixture on High for 4 hours. Then add tomato paste and mug beans. Stir the meal and cook it on high for 1 hour more.

Nutrition (per Serving): Calories 171 Protein 14g Carbs 5.4g Fat 9

Braised Beef

Prep Time: 8minutes | Cooking Time: 9 hours

Ingredients (2 Servings):

- 1 ½ lb. beef tenderloin, chopped
- 1 garlic clove, peeled
- 1 tsp peppercorn
- 1 tbsp dried basil
- 2 cups of water

Directions:

Put all ingredients from the list above in the slow cooker. Gently stir the mixture and close the lid. Cook the beef on low for 9 hours.

Nutrition (per Serving): Calories 522 Protein 44g Carbs 5.4g Fat 36

Coconut Beef

Prep Time: 10 minutes | Cooking Time: 8 hours

Ingredients (5 Servings):

- 1 lb. beef tenderloin, chopped
- 1 cup baby spinach, chopped
- 1 cup coconut milk
- 2 tsp avocado oil
- 2 tsp dried rosemary
- 2 tsp garlic powder

Directions:

Roast meat in the avocado oil for 1 minute per side on high heat. Ten transfer the meat in the slow cooker. Add garlic powder, dried rosemary, coconut milk, and baby spinach.

Close the lid and cook the meal on Low for 8 hours.

Nutrition (per Serving): Calories 288 Protein 18g Carbs 1.4g Fat 22.6

Beef Roast

Prep Time: 10 minutes | Cooking Time: 6 hours

Ingredients (5 Servings):

- 1 lb. beef chuck roast
- 1 tbsp ketchup
- 2 tbsp mayonnaise
- 1 tsp chili powder
- 2 tsp olive oil
- 2 tsp lemon juice
- ½ cup of water

Directions:

In the bowl mix ketchup, mayonnaise, chili powder, olive oil, and lemon juice. Then sprinkle the beef chuck roast with ketchup mixture. Pour the water in the slow cooker.

Add beef chuck roast and close the lid. Cook the meat on High for 6 hours.

Nutrition (per Serving): Calories 213 Protein 12.8g Carbs 7.4g Fat 17.1g

Lunch Beef

Prep Time: 10 minutes | Cooking Time: 8 hours

Ingredients (2 Servings):

- 1 lb. beef loin, chopped
- ½ white onion, sliced
- 1 tsp brown sugar
- 2 tsp chili powder
- 2 tsp hot sauce
- ½ cup okra, chopped
- 1 cup of water

Directions

Mix the beef loin with hot sauce, chili powder, and brown sugar. Transfer the meat in the slow cooker. Add water, okra, and onion. Cook the meal on Low for 8 hours.

Nutrition (per Serving): Calories 348 Protein 32.8g Carbs 1.4g Fat 24.1g

Braised Beef Strips

Prep Time: 10 minutes | Cooking Time: 5 hours

Ingredients (4 Servings):

- 1 lb. becf loin, cut into strips
- ½ cup mushroom, sliced
- 2 onion, sliced
- 1 cup water
- 2 tbsp coconut oil
- 1 tsp white pepper

Directions:

Melt the coconut oil in the skillet. Add mushrooms and roast them for 5 minutes on medium heat. Then transfer the mushrooms in the slow cooker. Add all remaining ingredients and close the lid. Cook the meal on High for 5 hours

Nutrition (per Serving): Calories 174 Protein 16.8g Carbs 2.4g Fat 13.1g

Beef Dip

Prep Time: 10 minutes | Cooking Time: 10 hours

Ingredients (6 Servings):

- 1 ½ lb. dried beef, chopped
- ½ cup heavy cream
- 1 onion, diced
- 2 tsp cream cheese
- ½ cup Cheddar cheese, shredded
- 2 tsp garlic powder

- ½ cup of water

Directions:

Put all ingredients in the slow cooker. Gently stir the ingredients and close the lid. Cook the dip on Low for 10 hours. Serve.

Nutrition (per Serving): Calories 313 Protein 19.4g Carbs 1.2g Fat 25.1g

Beef and Sauerkraut Bowl

Prep Time: 10 minutes | Cooking Time: 5 hours

Ingredients (4 Servings):

- 1 lb. corned beef, chopped
- 1 cup sauerkraut
- ¼ cup apple cider vinegar
- ½ cup water

Directions:

Pour water and apple cider vinegar in the slow cooker. Add corned beef and cook it on High for 5 hours. Then chop the meat roughly and put in the serving bowls. Top the meat with sauerkraut.

Nutrition (per Serving): Calories 202 Protein 15.5g Carbs 1.7g Fat 16.2g

Meatball Slow cooker

Prep Time: 15 minutes | Cooking Time: 2 hours

Ingredients (3 Servings):

For the meatballs:

- 1 lb. ground beef
- 2 tbsp tomato paste
- 1 cup bone broth
- 1 tsp paprika
- 1 tbsp cumin
- small handful fresh parsley, diced

For the cauliflower:

- 2 tbsp butter or ghee

- ½ large head cauliflower, florets

Directions:

Mix the meat, paprika, and cumin in a bowl. Form meatballs, then put it inside the slow cooker. Mix the paste and the broth in a bowl and pour over the meatballs. Cook on high, 2 hours. Steam the cauliflower florets until well cooked. Remove the water, then put butter. Blend the batter using an immersion blender until smooth. Mash the cauliflower onto a serving plate, top with meatballs, and sauce on top. Garnish with parsley and serve.

Nutrition (per Serving): Calories 313 Protein 26.7g Fat 23.4g Carbs 2.5g

Beef & Broccoli

Prep Time: 15 minutes | Cooking Time: 7 hours

Ingredients (4 Servings):

- 2 lb. flank steak, chunks
- 1 red bell pepper, sliced
- 1 broccoli, florets
- 1/4 tsp red pepper flakes
- 2 garlic cloves, minced
- 1 tsp grated ginger
- 3 tbsp sweetener
- 1 cup beef broth
- 2/3 cup coconut liquid
- 1 tsp sesame seeds, optional

Directions:

Set the slow cooker on low, put the steak, garlic, sweetener, beef broth, and coconut liquid. Cook within 5 to 6 hours. Mix the steak, then put in the red pepper plus the broccoli. Cook within 1 hour, then toss the batter. Serve with sesame seeds.

Nutrition (per Serving): Calories 357 Fat 49g Carbs 4g Protein 14g

Chili Colorado

Prep Time: 15 minutes | Cooking Time: 10 hours

Ingredients (12 Servings):

- 2.5 lb. beef
- 3 cloves garlic
- 20 oz green chilies, canned
- 1 tsp chili powder
- 2 onion
- 40 oz tomatoes, canned
- 1 tsp ground cumin

Directions:

Put the meat in the cooker. Add the garlic and onion. Add the tomatoes and chilies. Add the seasonings. Low cook for 10 hours. Serve.

Nutrition (per Serving): Calories 267 Fat 10g Protein 14 g Carbs 29g

Mississippi Roast

Prep Time: 15 minutes | Cooking Time: 8 hours

Ingredients (6 Servings):

- 2 lb. roast beef
- 1 pack dressing mix, ranch
- ½ cup butter, salted
- 3 tbsp olive oil
- 1 yellow onion, sliced
- 6 pepperoncini

Directions:

Sear the roast. Cover with chopped onion. Sprinkle ranch mix. Evenly disperse the butter. Evenly place pepperoncini. Low cook for 8 hours.

Nutrition (per Serving): Calories 368 Fat 31 g Protein 21.5g Carbs 2g

Beef Chimichangas

Prep Time: 15 minutes | Cooking Time: 12 hours

Ingredients (16 Servings):

- 3 lb. beef, boneless
- 10 oz green chilies and tomatoes, canned
- 2 tsp garlic powder
- 3 tbsp seasoning, taco
- 16 flour tortillas

Toppings:

- Refried beans
- Sour cream
- Guacamole
- Lettuce
- Cheese
- Salsa

Directions:

Prepare the meat. Add it to the cooker after applying seasoning. Add chilies and tomatoes. Toss in garlic Low cook for 12 hours. Shred the beef. Once removed, add it and all desired toppings to tortillas. Fry folded tortillas. Serve.

Nutrition (per Serving): Calories 179 Fat 10g Protein 14 g Carbs 6.6g

Artichoke and Peppers Beef

Prep Time: 10 minutes | Cooking Time: 6 hours

Ingredients (6 Servings):

- 2 lb. stew beef, cut into 1-inch cubes
- 12 oz artichoke hearts, drained
- 2 onion, diced
- 2 cup marinara sauce
- 1 tsp dried basil
- 2 tsp dried oregano

- 10 oz roasted red peppers, drained and sliced

Directions:

Add all ingredients into the cooking pot and stir well. Cover and cook on Low for 6 hours. Stir well and serve.

Nutrition (per Serving): Calories 343 Fat 18.6 g Carbs 15.8 g Protein 24.3 g

Italian Beef Roast

Prep Time: 10 minutes | Cooking Time: 6 hours

Ingredients (6 Servings):

- 2 lb. chuck roast, boneless
- 2 tbsp balsamic vinegar
- 2 tsp herbs de Provence
- 1/3 cup sun-dried tomatoes, chopped
- 8 garlic cloves, chopped
- 1/4 cup olives, chopped
- ½ cup chicken stock

Directions:

Add all ingredients into the cooking pot and stir well. Cover and cook on Low for 6 hours. Remove meat from pot and shred using a fork. Serve.

Nutrition (per Serving): Calories 329 Fat 25g Carbs 2.3 g Protein 21.1g

Olives and Feta Beef

Prep Time: 10 minutes | Cooking Time: 6 hours

Ingredients (6 Servings):

- 2 lb. beef stew meat, cut into half-inch pieces
- 1 cup olives, pitted and cut in half
- 30 oz can tomato, diced
- ½ cup feta cheese, crumbled
- ¼ tsp pepper

Directions:

Add all ingredients into the cooking pot and stir well. Cover and cook on High for 6 hours. Serve.

Nutrition (per Serving): Calories 779 Fat 54.5 g Carbs 49.2 g Protein 25g

Olives and Artichokes Beef

Prep Time: 10 minutes | Cooking Time: 7 hours

Ingredients (6 Servings):

- 2 lb. stew beef, cut into 1-inch cubes
- 1 tsp dried oregano
- ½ cup olives, pitted and chopped
- 12 oz can tomato, diced
- 12 oz can tomato sauce
- 32 oz beef stock
- ½ tsp ground cumin
- 1 tsp dried basil
- 3 garlic cloves, chopped
- 1 onion, diced
- 12 oz can artichoke hearts, drained and halved
- 2 tbsp olive oil

Directions:

Add the meat into the cooking pot then mix together the remaining ingredients and pour over the meat. Cover and cook on Low for 7 hours. Stir well and serve.

Nutrition (per Serving): Calories 587 Fat 36.2 g Carbs 54g Protein 26g

Sriracha Beef

Prep Time: 10 minutes | Cooking Time: 4 hours

Ingredients (6 Servings):

- 2 lb. beef chuck, sliced
- 1 ½ tbsp sriracha sauce
- 1/3 cup parsley, chopped

- 2 tsp garlic powder
- 1 cup beef broth
- 1 small onion, sliced
- 2 cups bell pepper, chopped

Directions:

Add the meat into the cooking pot then mix together the remaining ingredients and pour over the meat. Cover and cook on High for 4 hours. Stir well and serve.

Nutrition (per Serving): Calories 280 Fat 16. g Carbs 9.5 g Protein 27.5 g

Garlic Tomatoes Chuck Roast

Prep Time: 10 minutes | Cooking Time: 8 hours

Ingredients (6 Servings):

- 2 lb. beef chuck roast
- ½ cup beef broth
- ¼ cup sun-dried tomatoes, chopped
- 20 garlic cloves, peeled
- ¼ cup olives, sliced
- 2 tsp dried seasoning, crushed
- 2 tbsp balsamic vinegar

Directions:

Add the meat into the cooking pot then mix the remaining ingredients except for couscous and pour over the meat. Cover and cook on Low for 8 hours. Remove the meat from pot and shred using a fork. Return shredded meat to the pot and stir well.

Nutrition (per Serving): Calories 311 Fat 25g Carbs 2g Protein 21.8 g

Stuffed Bell Peppers

Prep Time: 10 minutes | Cooking Time: 4 hours

Ingredients (4 Servings):

- ½ lb. ground breakfast sausage

- 2 bell peppers, cut top and clean
- 6 large eggs
- 4 oz green chilies, chopped
- 4 oz jack cheese, shredded

Directions:

Brown sausage in a pan over medium heat. Drain excess grease. Pour 1/2 cup water in the cooking pot. In a bowl, whisk eggs until smooth. Stir green chilies, cheese, black pepper, and salt in eggs. Spoon egg mixture and brown sausage into each bell pepper. Place stuffed bell pepper in the cooking pot. Cover and cook on Low for 4 hours. Serve and enjoy.

Nutrition (per Serving): Calories 425 Fat 30.4 g Carbs 2.4 g Protein 36.7 g

Butter Beef

Prep Time: 10 minutes | Cooking Time: 8 hours

Ingredients (8 Servings):

- 3 lb. beef stew meat, cubed
- ½ cup butter
- 1 oz dry onion soup mix

Directions:

Place beef into the cooking pot and sprinkle with onion soup mix. Add butter over the beef. Cover and cook on Low for 8 hours. Stir well and serve.

Nutrition (per Serving): Calories 362 Fat 22.1g Carbs 2.3 g Protein 12g

S A L T & P E P P E R *the list of ingredient list do not indicate the amount of salt and pepper: you can add approximately a teaspoon of salt and, in if you like it, 1/2 teaspoon of pepper for each recipe*

CHAPTER 8: DESSERTS RECIPES

Hot Fudge Cake

Prep Time: 25 minutes | Cooking Time: 3 hours

Ingredients (10 Servings):

- 8 tbsp brown packed sugar
- 1 cup almond flour
- ¼ cup plus 3 tbsp unsweetened cocoa powder, divided
- 2 tsp baking powder
- ½ tsp salt
- ½ cup heavy cream
- 2 tbsp melted butter
- ½ tsp vanilla extract
- 2 cups boiling water

Directions:

Mix ¾ cup Sukrin Gold, almond flour, cocoa, baking powder, and salt. Stir in heavy cream, butter, and vanilla. Put it inside the slow cooker. Mix sugar and ¼ cup cocoa, then sprinkle over the mixture in the slow cooker. Pour in boiling water. Do not stir. Cook 2–3 hours, high. Serve.

Nutrition (per Serving): Calories 152 Fat 13 g Carbs 12 g Protein 4g

Fudgy Brownies

Prep Time: 10 minutes | Cooking Time: 2 hours

Ingredients (8 Servings):

- 4 large eggs
- 4 oz unsweetened chocolate
- ¾ cup of coconut oil
- ¾ cup frozen diced okra, partially thawed
- 30 stevia packets

- 1 tsp pure vanilla extract
- ¾ cup coconut flour
- ½–¾ cup coarsely chopped walnuts or pecans, optional

Directions:

Melt chocolate and coconut oil in a small saucepan. Put okra and eggs in a blender. Blend until smooth. Measure all other ingredients in the mixing bowl. Pour melted chocolate and okra over the dry ingredients and stir with a fork just until mixed. Pour into the greased slow cooker—cover and cook on high for 1½–2 hours.

Nutrition (per Serving): Calories 95 Fat 8 g Carbs 8g Protein 5g

Black and Blue Cobbler

Prep Time: 20 minutes | Cooking Time: 2 ½ hours

Ingredients (6 Servings):

- 2 eggs, beaten
- 1 cup almond flour
- 32 packets stevia, divided
- 1 tsp baking powder
- ¼ tsp ground cinnamon
- ¼ tsp ground nutmeg
- 2 tbsp whole milk
- 2 tbsp coconut oil, melted
- 2 cups fresh or frozen blueberries
- 2 cups fresh or frozen blackberries
- ¾ cup of water
- 2 tsp grated orange peel

Directions:

Combine almond flour, 18 packets stevia, baking powder, salt, cinnamon, and nutmeg. Combine eggs, milk, and oil. Stir into dry fixing.

Put it inside the greased slow cooker. Mix the berries, water, orange peel, and remaining 18 packets stevia in a saucepan. Bring to boil. Remove from heat and pour over batter. Cook on 2 hours, high. Let it cool within 30 minutes. Serve.

Nutrition (per Serving): Calories 194 Fat 16 g Carbs 21 g Protein 7 g

Chocolate Cheesecake

Prep Time: 15 minutes | Cooking Time: 2.5 hours

Ingredients (8 Servings):

- 3 cups cream cheese
- Pinch of salt
- 3 eggs
- 1 cup powder sweetener of your choice, Swerve (or a suitable substitute)
- 1 tsp vanilla extract
- ¼ cup sugarless dark chocolate chips

Directions:

Whisk the cream cheese, sweetener, and salt in a bowl. Add the eggs one at a time. Combine thoroughly. Spread the cheesecake in a cake pan, which fits in the slow cooker you are using.

Dissolved the chocolate chips in a small pot and pour over the batter. Using a knife, swirl the chocolate through the batter. Put 2 cups of water inside the slow cooker and set the cake pan inside. Cover it with a paper towel to absorb the water, then cook on high for 2.5 hours. Remove from the slow cooker and let it cool in the pan for 1 hour. Refrigerate.

Nutrition (per Serving): Calories 220 Carbs 8g Fat 19g Protein 12g

Crème Brulée

Prep Time: 15 minutes | Cooking Time: 2 hours

Ingredients (6 Servings):

- 6 large egg yolks
- 6 tbsp sweetener, Erythritol
- 2 cups double cream
- 1 Bourbon vanilla pod, scraped
- pinch of salt

Directions:

In a bowl, beat the eggs and sweetener together. Add the cream and vanilla. Whisk together.

Put it in one big dish. Set it in the slow cooker and pour hot water around- so the water reaches halfway up the dish. Cover, cook on high for 2 hours. Take the dishes out, let them cool. Refrigerate for 6-8 hours.

Nutrition (per Serving): Calories 187 Carbs 3g Fat 14g Protein 11g

Peanut Butter & Chocolate Cake

Prep Time: 15 minutes | Cooking Time: 4 hours

Ingredients (12 Servings):

- 4 large eggs
- 1 tbsp butter for greasing the slow cooker
- 2 cups almond flour
- ¾ cup sweetener of your choice
- ¼ cup coconut flakes
- ¼ cup whey protein powder
- 1 tsp baking powder
- ¼ tsp salt
- ¾ cup peanut butter, melted
- 1 tsp vanilla extract

- ½ cup of water
- 2 tbsp sugarless dark chocolate, melted

Directions:

Grease the slow cooker well. In a bowl, mix the dry ingredients. Stir in the wet ingredients one at a time. Spread about 2/3 of batter in the slow cooker, add half the chocolate. Swirl with a fork. Top up with the remaining batter and chocolate. Swirl again. Cook on low for 4 hours. Switch off. Let it sit covered for 30 minutes.

Nutrition (per Serving): Calories 270 Carbs 8g Fat 21g Protein 10g

Coconut Hot Chocolate

Prep Time: 15 minutes | Cooking Time: 4 hours

Ingredients (8 Servings):
- 4 ½ cups full-fat coconut milk
- 2 cups heavy cream
- 1 tsp vanilla extract
- 1/3 cup cocoa powder
- 3 oz dark chocolate, roughly chopped
- ½ tsp cinnamon
- few drops of stevia to taste

Directions:

Add the coconut milk, cream, vanilla extract, cocoa powder, chocolate, cinnamon, and stevia to the slow cooker and stir to combine. Cook for 4 hours, high, whisking every 45 minutes. Taste the hot chocolate and if you prefer more sweetness, add a few more drops of stevia.

Nutrition (per Serving): Calories 537 Carbs 17g Fat 54g Protein 6.5g

Yogurt and Berries bowl

Prep Time: 15 minutes | Cooking Time: 3 hours

Ingredients (10 Servings):

- 1 cup unsweetened shredded coconut
- ¾ cup slivered almonds
- 2 oz dark chocolate (high cocoa percentage), roughly chopped
- 1/3 cup pumpkin seeds
- 2 oz salted butter
- 1 tsp cinnamon
- 2 cups heavy cream
- 2 cups full-fat Greek yogurt
- 1 cup fresh berries

Directions:

Place the shredded coconut, slivered almonds, dark chocolate, pumpkin seeds, butter, and cinnamon into the slow cooker. Cook for 3 hours, high, stirring every 45 minutes to combine the chocolate and butter as it melts. Remove the mixture from the slow cooker, place in a bowl, and leave to cool. In a large bowl, whip the cream until softly whipped. Stir the yogurt through the cream. Slice the strawberries into pieces, then put it to the cream mixture, along with the other berries you are using, fold through. Sprinkle the cooled coconut mixture over the cream mixture.

Nutrition (per Serving): Calories 387 Carbs 16g Fat 39g Protein 7g

Dark Chocolate & Peppermint Pots

Prep Time: 15 minutes | Cooking Time: 2 hours

Ingredients (4 Servings):
- 2 cups heavy cream
- 3 oz dark chocolate, melted in the microwave
- 4 egg yolks, lightly beaten with a fork
- few drops of stevia
- few drops of peppermint essence to taste

Directions:

Mix the beaten egg yolks, cream, stevia, melted chocolate, and peppermint essence in a medium-sized bowl. Prepare the pots by greasing 6 ramekins with butter.

Pour the chocolate mixture into the pots evenly. Put the pots inside the slow cooker and put hot water below halfway up. Cook for 2 hours, high. Take the pots out of the slow cooker and leave to cool and set. Serve with a fresh mint leaf and whipped cream.

Nutrition (per Serving): Calories 555 Carbs 11g Fat 54g Protein 6.4g

Creamy Vanilla Custard

Prep Time: 15 minutes | Cooking Time: 3 hours

Ingredients (6 Servings):

- 3 cups full-fat cream
- 4 egg yolks, lightly beaten
- 2 tsp vanilla extract
- few drops of stevia

Directions:

Mix the cream, egg yolks, vanilla extract, and stevia in a medium-sized bowl. Pour the mixture into a heat-proof dish. Place the dish into the slow cooker. Put hot water into the pot, around the dish, halfway up. Set the temperature to high. Cook for 3 hours. Serve hot or cold!

Nutrition (per Serving): Calories 236 Carbs 3g Fat 17g Protein 14g

Coconut and Chocolate Truffle Bake

Prep Time: 15 minutes | Cooking Time: 4 hours

Ingredients (8 Servings):

- 3 oz butter, melted
- 2 oz dark chocolate, melted

- 1 cup ground almonds
- 1 cup dehydrated coconut
- 3 tbsp unsweetened cocoa powder
- 2 tsp vanilla extract
- 1 ½ cup heavy cream
- a few extra squares of dark chocolate, grated
- ¼ cup toasted almonds, chopped

Directions:

In a large bowl, mix the melted butter, chocolate, ground almonds, coconut, cocoa powder, and vanilla extract. Roll the mixture into balls. Grease a heat-proof dish. Place the balls into the dish—Cook for 4 hours, low setting. Leave the truffle dish to cool until warm. Mix the cream until you make a soft peak. Spread the cream over the truffle dish and sprinkle the grated chocolate and chopped toasted almonds over the top. Serve immediately!

Nutrition (per Serving): Calories 415 Carbs 17g Fat 35g Protein 8g

Peanut Butter, Chocolate & Pecan Cupcakes

Prep Time: 15 minutes | Cooking Time: 4 hours

Ingredients (14 Servings):

- 14 paper cupcake cases
- 1 ½ cup smooth peanut butter
- 2 oz butter
- 2 tsp vanilla extract
- 3 oz dark chocolate
- 2 tbsp coconut oil
- 2 eggs, beaten
- 1 cup ground almonds
- 1 tsp baking powder
- 1 tsp cinnamon

- 12 pecan nuts, toasted and finely chopped

Directions:

Dissolve the dark chocolate plus coconut oil in the microwave, stir to combine, and set aside.

Place the peanut butter and butter into a medium-sized bowl, microwave for 30 seconds at a time until the butter has just melted. Mix the peanut butter plus butter until combined and smooth. Stir the vanilla extract into the peanut butter mixture. Mix the ground almonds, eggs, baking powder, and cinnamon in a small bowl. Pour the melted chocolate and coconut oil evenly into the 14 paper cases. Spoon half of the almond/egg mixture evenly into the cases, on top of the chocolate and press down slightly. Spoon the peanut butter mixture into the cases, on top of the almond/egg mixture. Spoon the remaining almond/egg mixture into the cases. Put the pecans on top of each cupcake. Put the filled cases into the slow cooker—Cook for 4 hours, high setting.

Nutrition (per Serving): Calories 258 Carbs 8.8g Fat 22g Protein 9g

Vanilla & Strawberry Cheesecake

Prep Time: 15 minutes | Cooking Time: 6 hours

Ingredients (8 Servings):

Base:

- 2 oz butter, melted
- 1 cup ground hazelnuts
- ½ cup dehydrated coconut
- 2 tsp vanilla extract
- 1 tsp cinnamon

Filling:

- 2 cups cream cheese

- 2 eggs, beaten
- 1 cup sour cream
- 2 tsp vanilla extract
- 8 large strawberries, chopped

Directions:

Mix the melted butter, hazelnuts, coconut, vanilla, and cinnamon in a medium-sized bowl. Press the base into a greased heat-proof dish.

Mix the cream cheese, eggs, sour cream, and vanilla extract, beat with electric eggbeaters in a large bowl until thick and combined. Fold the strawberries through the cream cheese mixture. Put the cream cheese batter into the dish, on top of the base, spread out until smooth. Put it in the slow cooker and put hot water around the dish until halfway up. Cook for 6 hours, low setting until just set but slightly wobbly. Chill before serving.

Nutrition (per Serving): Calories 256 Carbs 8g Fat 21g Protein 10g

Coffee Creams with Topping

Prep Time: 15 minutes | Cooking Time: 4 hours

Ingredients (6 Servings):

- 2 cups heavy cream
- 4 egg yolks, lightly beaten
- 1 tsp vanilla extract
- 4 tbsp strong espresso coffee (or 3tsp instant coffee dissolved in 3tbsp boiling water)
- ½ cup mixed seeds – sesame seeds, pumpkin seeds, chia seeds, sunflower seeds,
- 1 tsp cinnamon
- 2 tbsp coconut oil

Directions:

Heat-up the coconut oil in a small frypan until melted. Add the mixed seeds, cinnamon, and a pinch of salt, toss in the oil and heat until toasted and golden, place into a small bowl and set aside. Mix the cream, egg yolks, vanilla, and coffee in a medium-sized bowl.

Pour the cream/coffee mixture into the ramekins. Place the ramekins into the slow cooker. Put hot water inside until halfway. Cook on low setting for 4 hours. Remove, then leave to cool slightly on the bench. Sprinkle the seed mixture over the top of each custard before serving.

Nutrition (per Serving): Calories 315 Carbs 4g Fat 32g Protein 3g

Lemon Cheesecake

Prep Time: 15 minutes | Cooking Time: 6 hours

Ingredients (10 Servings):

- 3 eggs, lightly beaten
- 2 oz butter, melted
- 1 ½ cup pecans, finely ground in the food processor
- 1 tsp cinnamon
- 2 cups cream cheese
- 1 cup sour cream
- 1 lemon
- few drops of stevia
- 1 cup heavy cream

Directions:

Mix the melted butter, ground pecans, and cinnamon until it forms a wet, sand-like texture. Press the butter/pecan mixture into a greased, heat-proof dish and set aside.

Place the cream cheese, eggs, sour cream, stevia, zest, and juice of one lemon into a large bowl, beat with electric eggbeaters until combined and smooth.

Put the cream cheese batter into the dish, on top of the base. Place the dish inside the slow

cooker, then put warm water in halfway up. Cook within 6 hours, low setting. Set the cheesecake on the bench to cool and set. Whip the cream until soft peak and spread over the cheesecake before serving.

Nutrition (per Serving): Calories 371 Carbs 5g Fat 36g Protein 9,5g

Avocado and Mango Bowls

Prep Time: 10 minutes | Cooking Time: 2 hours

Ingredients (2 Servings):

- 1 cup avocado, peeled, pitted and cubed
- 1 cup mango, peeled and cubed
- 2 apple, cored and cubed
- 2 tbsp brown sugar
- 1 cup heavy cream
- 2 tbsp lemon juice

Directions:

In your slow cooker, combine the avocado with the mango and the other ingredients, toss gently, put the lid on and cook on Low for 2 hours. Divide the mix into bowls and serve.

Nutrition (per Serving): Calories 580 Fat 55g Carbs 23g Protein 4.4g

Ricotta Cream

Prep Time: 2 H 10 minutes |Cooking Time: 1 hour

Ingredients (10 Servings):

- ½ cup hot coffee
- 1 ½ cup ricotta cheese
- ½ tsp gelatin
- 1 tsp vanilla extract
- 1 tsp espresso powder
- 1 tsp sugar
- 1 cup whipping cream

Directions:

In a bowl, mix coffee with gelatin, stir well and leave aside until coffee is cold. In your slow cooker, mix espresso, sugar, vanilla extract and ricotta and stir. Add coffee mix and whipping cream, cover, cook on Low for 1 hour. Divide into dessert bowls and keep in the fridge for 2 hours before serving.

Nutrition (per Serving): Calories 116 Fat 13g Carbs 2g Protein 5g

Tomato Jam

Prep Time: 10 minutes | Cooking Time: 3 hours

Ingredients (2 Servings):

- ½ lb. tomatoes, chopped
- 1 green apple, grated
- 2 tbsp red wine vinegar
- 2 tbsp sugar

Directions:

In your slow cooker, mix the tomatoes with the apple with the other ingredients, put the lid on and cook on Low for 3 hours. Whisk the jam well, blend a bit using an immersion blender, divide into bowls and serve cold.

Nutrition (per Serving): Calories 70 Fat 1g Carbs 14g Protein 1g

Green Tea Pudding

Prep Time: 10 minutes | Cooking Time: 1 hour

Ingredients (2 Servings):

- ½ cup coconut milk
- 1 ½ cup avocado, pitted and peeled
- 1 tbsp green tea powder
- 1 tsp lime zest, grated
- 1 tbsp sugar

Directions:

In your slow cooker, mix coconut milk with avocado, tea powder, lime zest and sugar, stir, cover and cook on Low for 1 hour. Divide into cups and serve cold.

Nutrition (per Serving): Calories 297 Fat 27g Carbs 10.9g Protein 3.5g

Sweet Lemon Mix

Prep Time: 5 minutes | Cooking Time: 1 hour

Ingredients (4 Servings):

- ½ cup heavy cream
- sugar to the taste
- lemons, peeled and roughly chopped

Directions:

In your slow cooker, mix cream with sugar and lemons, stir, cover and cook on Low for 1 hour. Divide into glasses and serve very cold.

Nutrition (per Serving): Calories 107 Fat 11g Carbs 1g Protein 1g

Coconut Jam

Prep Time: 10 minutes | Cooking Time: 3 hours

Ingredients (2 Servings):

- ½ cup coconut flesh, shredded
- 1 cup coconut cream
- ½ cup heavy cream
- 2 tbsp sugar
- 1 tbsp lemon juice

Directions:

In your slow cooker, mix the coconut cream with the lemon juice, add other ingredients, whisk, put the lid on and cook on Low for 2 hours. Whisk well, divide into bowls and serve cold.

Nutrition (per Serving): Calories 570 Fat 51g Carbs 25g Protein 9g

Banana Bread

Prep Time: 10 minutes | Cooking Time: 3 hours

Ingredients (6 Servings):

- 2 eggs
- ¾ cup sugar
- 1/3 cup butter, soft
- 1 tsp vanilla extract
- 2 bananas, mashed
- 1 tsp baking powder
- 1 ½ cups flour
- ½ tsp baking soda
- 1/3 cup milk
- 1 ½ tsp cream of tartar
- cooking spray

Directions:

In a bowl, combine milk with cream of tartar and stir well.

Add sugar, butter, egg, vanilla and bananas and stir everything. In another bowl, mix flour with salt, baking powder and soda. Combine the 2 mixtures and stir them well.

Grease your slow cooker with cooking spray, add bread batter, cover, and cook on High for 3 hours. Leave the bread to cool down, slice and serve it.

Nutrition (per Serving): Calories 271 Fat 12g Carbs 33g Protein 6g

Bread and Berries Pudding

Prep Time: 10 minutes | Cooking Time: 3 hours

Ingredients (2 Servings):

- 1 ½ cups white bread, cubed
- 1 cup blackberries

- 1 tbsp butter, melted
- 1 tbsp white sugar
- 1 cup almond milk
- ¼ cup heavy cream
- 2 eggs, whisked
- 1 tbsp lemon zest, grated
- ¼ tsp vanilla extract

Directions:

In your slow cooker, mix the bread with the berries, butter and the other ingredients, toss gently, put the lid on and cook on Low for 3 hours. Divide pudding between dessert plates and serve.

Nutrition (per Serving): Calories 324 Fat 23g Carbs 20g Protein 9g

Candied Lemon

Prep Time: 20 minutes | Cooking Time: 4 hours

Ingredients (4 Servings):

- 2 lemons, peeled and cut into medium segments
- ½ cup white sugar
- 1 cup water

Directions:

In your slow cooker, mix lemons with sugar and water, cover, cook on Low for 4 hours, transfer them to bowls and serve cold.

Nutrition (per Serving): Calories 218 Fat 0g Carbs 55g Protein 0g

Tapioca and Chia Pudding

Prep Time: 10 minutes | Cooking Time: 3 hours

Ingredients (2 Servings):

- 1 cup almond milk
- ¼ cup tapioca pearls
- 1 tbsp chia seeds

- 2 eggs, whisked
- ½ tsp vanilla extract
- 1 tbsp sugar
- ½ tbsp lemon zest, grated

Directions:

In your slow cooker, mix the tapioca pearls with the milk, put the lid on and cook on Low for 3 hours. Divide the pudding into bowls and serve cold.

Nutrition (per Serving): Calories 110 Fat 6g Carbs 5g Protein 6g

Chocolate and Liquor Cream

Prep Time: 10 minutes | Cooking Time: 2 hours

Ingredients (4 Servings):

- 12 oz crème fraiche
- 10 oz dark chocolate, cut into chunks1 tsp liquor
- 1 tsp sugar

Directions:

In your slow cooker mix crème fraiche with chocolate, liquor and sugar, stir, cover, cook on Low for 2 hours. Divide into bowls and serve cold.

Nutrition (per Serving): Calories 670 Fat 56g Carbs 48g Protein 9g

Dates and Rice Pudding

Prep Time: 10 minutes | Cooking Time: 3 hours

Ingredients (2 Servings):

- 1 cup dates, chopped
- ½ cup white rice
- 1 cup almond milk
- 2 tbsp brown sugar
- 1 tsp almond extract

Directions:

In your slow cooker, mix the rice with the milk and the other ingredients, whisk, put the lid on and cook on Low for 3 hours. Divide the pudding into bowls and serve.

Nutrition (per Serving): Calories 332 Fat 2,5g Carb 81g Protein 3.5g

Butternut Squash and Sweet Mix

Prep Time: 10 minutes | Cooking Time: 2 hours

Ingredients (8 Servings):

- ½ lb. butternut squash, steamed, peeled and mashed
- 2 large eggs
- 1 cup milk
- ¾ cup maple syrup
- 1 tsp cinnamon powder
- ½ tsp ginger powder
- ¼ tsp cloves, ground
- 1 tbsp cornstarch
- whipped cream to serve

Directions:

In a bowl, mix squash with maple syrup, milk, eggs, cinnamon, cornstarch, ginger, and cloves and stir very well. Pour this into your slow cooker, cover, cook on Low for 2 hours, divide into cups and serve with whipped cream on top.

Nutrition (per Serving): Calories 91 Fat 5g Carbs 10g Protein 4g

Almonds, Walnuts & Mango Bowls

Prep Time: 10 minutes | Cooking Time: 2 hours

Ingredients (2 Servings):

- 1/2 cup walnuts, chopped
- 3 tbsp almonds, chopped
- 1 cup mango, peeled and roughly cubed

- 1 cup heavy cream
- ½ tsp vanilla extract
- 1 tsp almond extract
- 2 tbsp brown sugar

Directions:

In your slow cooker, mix the walnuts with the mango, cream and the other ingredients, toss, put the lid on and cook on High for 2 hours. Divide the mix into bowls and serve.

Nutrition (per Serving): Calories 664 Fat 64g Carbs 24g Protein 9g

Tapioca Pudding

Prep Time: 10 minutes | Cooking Time: 1 hour

Ingredients (6 Servings):

- 1 ¼ cups milk
- 1/3 cup tapioca pearls, rinsed
- ½ cup water
- ½ cup sugar
- zest of ½ lemon

Directions:

In your slow cooker, mix tapioca with milk, sugar, water and lemon zest, stir, cover, cook on Low for 1 hour, divide into cups and serve warm.

Nutrition (per Serving): Calories 130 Fat 4g Carbs 21g Protein 3g

Berries Salad

Prep Time: 10 minutes | Cooking Time: 1 hour

Ingredients (2 Servings):

- ½ cup heavy cream
- 2 tbsp brown sugar
- 1 tbsp lime juice
- 1 tbsp lime zest, grated
- 1 cup blueberries
- ½ cup cranberries
- 1 cup blackberries
- 1 cup strawberries

Directions:

In your slow cooker, mix the berries with the sugar and the other ingredients, toss, put the lid on and cook on High for 1 hour. Divide the mix into bowls and serve.

Nutrition (per Serving): Calories 262 Fat 22g Carbs 13g Protein 3g

Fresh Cream Mix

Prep Time: 1 hour | Cooking Time: 1 hour

Ingredients (6 Servings):

- 1 ½ cup fresh cream
- 1 tsp cinnamon powder
- 3 egg yolks
- 2 tbsp white sugar
- Zest of 1 orange, grated
- a pinch of nutmeg for serving
- 2 tbsp sugar
- 1 ½ cup water

Directions:

In a bowl, mix cream, cinnamon and orange zest and stir. In another bowl, mix the egg yolks with white sugar and whisk well. Add this over the cream, stir, strain and divide into ramekins. Put ramekins in your slow cooker, add 2 cups water to the slow cooker, cover, cook on Low for 1 hour, leave cream aside to cool down and serve.

Nutrition (per Serving): Calories 136 Fat 10g Carbs 4g Protein 8g

Pears and Apples Bowls

Prep Time: 10 minutes | Cooking Time: 2 hours

Ingredients (2 Servings):

- 1 tsp vanilla extract
- 2 pears, cored and cut into wedges
- 2 apples, cored and cut into wedges
- 1 tbsp walnuts, chopped
- 2 tbsp brown sugar
- ½ cup coconut cream

Directions:

In your slow cooker, mix the pears with the apples, nuts and the other ingredients, toss, put the lid on and cook on Low for 2 hours. Divide the mix into bowls and serve cold.

Nutrition (per Serving): Calories 366 Fat 24g Carbs 41 g Protein 3 g

Macadamia Fudge Truffles

Prep Time: 15 minutes | Cooking Time: 4 hours

Ingredients (25 Servings):

- 1 cup roasted macadamia nuts, finely chopped
- ½ cup ground almonds
- 2 oz butter, melted
- 6 oz dark chocolate, melted
- 1 tsp vanilla extract
- 1 egg, lightly beaten

Directions:

Place the macadamia nuts, almonds, melted butter, melted chocolate, vanilla, and egg into a large bowl, stir until combined. Grease the bottom of the slow cooker by rubbing with butter. Place the mixture into the slow cooker and press down. Set to cook low setting within 4 hours.

Allow the batter to cool until just warm. Take a tsp, scoop the mixture out, and roll into balls.

Refrigerate to harden slightly. Store the truffle balls in the fridge.

Nutrition (per Serving): Calories 92 Carbs 6g Fat 7.6g Protein 2g

Chocolate Covered Bacon Cupcakes

Prep Time: 15 minutes | Cooking Time: 3 hours

Ingredients (10 Servings):

- 10 paper cupcake cases
- 5 slices streaky bacon, cut into small pieces, fried in a pan until crispy
- 6 oz dark chocolate, melted
- 1 cup ground hazelnuts
- 1 tsp baking powder
- 2 eggs, lightly beaten
- ½ cup full-fat Greek yogurt
- 1 tsp vanilla extract

Directions:

Mix the fried bacon pieces and melted chocolate in a bowl, set aside.

Mix the ground hazelnuts, baking powder, eggs, yogurt, vanilla, and a pinch of salt in a medium-sized bowl. Spoon the hazelnut mixture into the cupcake cases. Spoon the chocolate and bacon mixture on top of the hazelnut mixture. Place the cupcake cases into the slow cooker. Cook for 3 hours, high setting. Remove the cupcakes from the pot and leave to cool on the bench before storing serving. Serve with whipped cream!

Nutrition (per Serving): Calories 201 Carbs 13g Fat 15g Protein 5.4g

Chocolate, Berry, And Macadamia Jars

Prep Time: 15 minutes | Cooking Time: 6 hours

Ingredients (6 Servings):

- 6 oz dark chocolate, melted
- ½ cup mixed berries, (fresh) – any berries you like
- 3/4 cup toasted macadamia nuts, chopped
- 6 oz cream cheese
- ½ cup heavy cream
- 1 tsp vanilla extract

Directions

Whisk the cream cheese, cream, and vanilla extract in a medium-sized bowl.

Scoop a small amount of melted chocolate, put it into each jar or ramekin. Place a few berries on top of the chocolate. Sprinkle some toasted macadamias onto the berries. Scoop the cream cheese mixture into the ramekin. Place another layer of chocolate, berries, and macadamia nuts on top of the cream cheese mixture. Put the jars inside the slow cooker and put the hot water until it reaches halfway up. Set to low, then cook for 6 hours.

Remove the jars and leave them to cool and set on the bench for about 2 hours before serving.

Nutrition (per Serving): Calories 400 Carbs 25g Fat 35g Protein 6g

Choco-peanut Cake

Prep Time: 15 minutes | Cooking Time: 2 hours

Ingredients (10 Servings):

- 14 oz pudding type mix
- 1 cup of water
- ½ cup salted butter, melted
- 3 eggs
- 6 oz peanut butter

For the topping

- 1 cup creamy peanut butter
- 3 tbsp powdered sugar
- 10 bite-size Reese's peanut butter cups

Directions:

Mix the cake mixture, ice, butter, and eggs in a large bowl until smooth. Some lumps are all right, that's all right. Cut the cups of the mini peanut butter. Cleaner non-stick spray on the slow cooker. Add the butter slowly and spread over an even layer. Cover and cook on high during the cooking time for 2 hours without opening the lid. Melt the peanut butter over medium heat in a pan. Stir until melted and smooth; observe as it burns hard. To smooth, add the powdered sugar and whisk. Pour over the butter of the sweetened peanut in the cake, then serve.

Nutrition (per Serving): Calories 457 Carbs 27g Protein 13g Fat 44g

Slow cooker Apple Pudding Cake

Prep Time: 15 minutes | Cooking Time: 3 hours

Ingredients (10 Servings):

- 2 cups all-purpose flour
- 2/3 plus 1/4 cup sugar, divided
- 3 tsp baking powder
- 1 tsp salt
- ½ cup butter cold
- 1 ½ cup milk
- 4 apples, diced
- 1 ½ cups orange juice
- ½ cup honey
- 2 tbsp butter melted
- 2 tsp cinnamon

Directions:

Mix the flour, 2/3 cup sugar, baking powder, and salt. Slice the butter until you have coarse crumbs in the mixture. Remove the milk from the crumbs until moistened. Grease a 4 or 5 qt slow cooker's bottom and sides. Spoon the batter into the slow cooker's bottom and spread evenly. Place the diced apples evenly over the mixture. Whisk together the orange juice, honey, butter, remaining sugar, and cinnamon in a medium-sized pan. Garnish the apples.

Place the slow cooker opening with a clean kitchen towel, place the lid on, it prevents condensation from reaching the slow cooker from the cover. Place the slow cooker on top and cook until apples are tender for 2 to 3 hours. Serve hot.

Nutrition (per Serving): Calories 345 Fat 9g Carbs 49g Protein 4.3g

Slow cooker Brownie Cookies

Prep Time: 15 minutes | Cooking Time: 2 hours

Ingredients (10 Servings):

- 1 box brownie mix
- 3 eggs
- ¼ cup butter melted
- ½ cup mini chocolate chips
- ½ cup chopped walnuts optional
- 10 cookie dough slices

Directions:

Combine your brownie mixture with butter, eggs, chocolate chips, and nuts.

Sprinkle with non-stick spray the inside of your slow cooker. Place eight slices of ready-made cookie dough or pile tbsp of it on the bottom. In your slow cooker, pour brownie mixture on top and smooth out evenly. Put on the lid and cook on top for 2 hours. To get both textures in

your meal, scoop from the middle out to the edge for each serving. If desired, serve warm for best results, top with ice cream.

Nutrition (per Serving): Calories 160 Fat 12g Carbs 9g Protein 5g

Slow cooker Chocolate Caramel Monkey Bread

Prep Time: 15 minutes | Cooking Time: 1 H

Ingredients (6 Servings):

- 1 tbsp sugar
- 1/4 tsp ground cinnamon
- 15 oz buttermilk biscuits
- 18 milk chocolate-covered caramels
- caramel sauce for topping (optional)
- chocolate sauce for topping (optional)

Directions

Mix sugar and cinnamon and set aside. Fill a parchment paper slow cooker, cover up to the bottom. Wrap 1 buttermilk biscuit dough around one chocolate candy to cover the candy completely, pinching the seam closed. Place the biscuit-wrapped candy in the slow cooker bottom, start in the middle of the slow cooker and work your way to the sides. Continue to wrap candy and put it in the slow cooker, leaving roughly 1/2 inch between each. Repeat these steps with sweets wrapped in the second layer of biscuit. Sprinkle the remaining cinnamon-sugar mixture on top when using all the dough and confectionery.

Cover the slow cooker and cook for 1 1/2 hours on the lower side. Once cooked, remove the lid and let cool slightly. Use the edges of the parchment paper to lift the monkey bread out of the slow cooker. Allow cooling for at least 10-15 minutes. Cut off any excess parchment paper around the edge when ready to serve. In a shallow bread or bowl, put monkey bread and drizzle with chocolate and caramel sauces.

Nutrition (per Serving): Calories 277 Fat 16g Carbs 30g Protein 5g

Slow Cooked Coffee Cake

Prep Time: 15 minutes | Cooking Time: 2 H 30 minutes

Ingredients (6 Servings):

- 2 eggs
- 2 cups all-purpose flour
- 1 cups brown sugar
- 2/3 cup vegetable oil
- 1 1/3 cups almond milk
- 2 tsp baking powder
- ½ tsp baking soda
- 1 tsp ground cinnamon
- 1 tsp white vinegar
- 1 tsp salt
- ½ cup chopped nuts optional

Directions:

In a large bowl, whisk in flour, brown sugar, and salt. Remove the oil until it is crumbly mixed.

In the flour mixture, combine the baking powder, baking soda, and cinnamon with a wooden spoon or spatula. In a measuring cup, place milk, oil, eggs, and vinegar and whisk, then add to the flour mixture and stir until mixed. Spray a non-stick cooking spray 5-7qt slow cooker or line with a slow cooker liner. Pour into it with the batter. Sprinkle the cake batter's nuts over the end. Put a paper towel over the slow cooker insert and place the lid on top of it. Cook within 1 hour, high or 2 hours on low.

Serve warm directly from the slow cooker or store for up to 3 days in an airtight container.

Nutrition (per Serving): Calories 365 Carbs 66g Protein 9g Fat 9g

Slow cooker Apple Pear Crisp

Prep Time: 15 minutes | Cooking Time: 4 hours

Ingredients (8 Servings):

- 4 apples, peeled and cut into 1/2-inch slices
- 4 pears, peeled and cut into 1/2-inch slices
- 1/3 cup light brown sugar
- 1 tbsp all-purpose flour
- 1 tbsp lemon juice
- ½ tsp ground cinnamon
- 1/4 tsp salt
- Pinch of ground nutmeg

For the Topping:

- 3/4 cup all-purpose flour
- 3/4 cup old fashioned oats
- ½ cup chopped pecans
- 1/3 cup light brown sugar
- ½ tsp ground cinnamon
- ½ tsp salt
- 8 tbsp unsalted butter, cut into cubes

Directions:

Combine flour, oats, pecans, sugar, cinnamon, and salt to make the topping. Press the butter into the dry fixing until it looks like coarse crumbs; set aside.

Coat lightly with a non-stick spray inside a 4-qt slow cooker: put apples and pears in the slow cooker. Add brown sugar, flour, juice of lemon, cinnamon, salt, and nutmeg. Sprinkle with reserved topping, gently pressing the crumbs into the butter using your fingertips. Layer the slow cooker with a clean dishtowel. Cover and cook for 2-3 hours at low heat or 90 minutes at high temperature, remove the dishtowel and continue to cook, uncovered until the top is browned and apples are tender for about 1 hour. Serve cold.

Nutrition (per Serving): Calories 323 Carbs 47g Protein 3g Fat 17g

Key Lime Dump Cake Recipe

Prep Time: 15 minutes | Cooking Time: 2 hours

Ingredients (10 Servings):

- 14 oz French Vanilla Cake Mix box
- 40 oz Key Lime Pie Filling
- 8 tbsp or ½ cup butter melted

Directions:

Spray inside the Slow cooker with a non-stick cooking spray. Empty key lime pie cans filling in the Slow cooker bottom and then spread evenly. Mix the dry vanilla cake mix with the dissolved butter in a bowl. Pour the crumble cake/butter mixture over the slow cooker, spread evenly, and cover the slow cooker with the lid. Cook for 2 hours at high or 4 hours at low. serve with ice cream or whip cream.

Nutrition (per Serving): Calories 501 Carbs 74g Protein 2.7g Fat 24g

Slow cooker Cherry Cake

Prep Time: 15 minutes | Cooking Time: 2 hours

Ingredients (10 Servings):

- 14 oz Devil's Food Cake Mix
- 42 oz Cherry Pie Filling
- ½ cup butter melted

Directions:

Spray with a non-stick cooking spray inside the slow cooker. Empty cherry pie filling cans into slow cooker's bottom, then evenly spread out. Combine dry cake mix with butter in a medium bowl. Pour the crumble cake/butter mixture over the slow cooker plus cherries, scatter evenly, and cover the slow cooker with a lid.

Cook for 2 hours at high, or 4 hours at low. Use ice cream or whip cream to serve.

Nutrition (per Serving): Calories 477 Fat 20.8g Carbs 65g Protein 3g

Slow cooker Pumpkin Spice Cake Recipe

Prep Time: 15 minutes | Cooking Time: 2 hours

Ingredients (10 Servings):

- 14 oz Spice Cake Mix
- 14 oz Pure Pumpkin
- ½ cup Applesauce
- 3 eggs
- 2 tsp Pumpkin Pie Spice

Directions:

Whisk all the fixing with a mixer for 1 minute. Spray with nonstick cooking spray inside the slow cooker. Pour over and cover the mixture into the slow cooker. Cook for 1.5 – 2 hours or until finished. Serve.

Nutrition (per Serving): Calories 189 Fat 3g Carbs 37g Protein 4g

Slow cooker Blueberry Dump Cake Recipe

Prep Time: 15 minutes | Cooking Time: 2 hours

Ingredients (10 Servings):

- 14 oz Lemon Cake Mix
- 40 oz Blueberry Pie Filling

- ½ cup butter melted

Directions:

Spray with non-stick cooking spray the slow cooker. Put blueberry pie filling evenly into the bottom of the slow cooker. In a mixing bowl, combine dry lemon cake mix with melted butter and stir until crumbly. Break some big chunks into the crumbles of a small spoon.

Pour the crumble cake/butter mixture over the blueberry mixture into slow cooker, spread evenly, and cover with a lid the slow cooker.

Cook at high for 2 hours, and at low for 4 hours. Serve.

Nutrition (per Serving): Calories 424 Fat 9g Carbs 82g Protein 2.26g

Slow cooker Strawberry Dump Cake Recipe

Prep Time: 15 minutes | Cooking Time: 2 hours

Ingredients (10 Servings):

- 14 oz Strawberry Cake Mix
- 40 oz Strawberry Pie Filling
- ½ cup butter melted

Directions:

Spray with a non-stick cooking spray inside the slow cooker. Put the Strawberry Pie Filling into the slow cooker's bottom and spread evenly. Combine strawberry dry cake mixture with the butter in a mixing bowl. Pour the cake/butter crumbled mixture into slow cooker over strawberries and spread evenly, covering the slow cooker with a lid. Cook for 2 hours at high, or 4 hours at low. Serve.

Nutrition (per Serving): Calories 401 Fat 11.5g Carbs 56g Protein 1.8g

Sugar-Free Chocolate Cake

Prep Time: 15 minutes | Cooking Time: 3 hours

Ingredients (3 Servings):

- 2 egg yolk
- 1 whole egg
- ½ cup hot water
- 1 oz chocolate chips, sugar-free
- 1/4 tsp stevia
- 1/4 tsp vanilla extract
- 2 tbsp butter melted, cooled
- 1/4 tsp baking powder
- 1/8 tsp salt
- 3 tsp cocoa powder, unsweetened
- 2 tbsp almond flour
- 6 tbsp Swerve sweetener divided

Directions:

Grease the slow cooker, mix the flour, baking powder, 2 tbsp cocoa powder, almond flour, and 4 tbsp of Swerve in a bowl. In a separate bowl, stir in eggs with melted butter, liquid stevia, vanilla extract, egg yolks, and eggs. Mix the wet fixing to the dry ones and combine to incorporate fully. Pour the mixture into the slow cooker. Top the mixture with chocolate chips. Mix the remaining swerve with cocoa powder and hot water in a separate bowl and pour this mixture over chocolate chips. Cook on low within 3 hours. Once done, let cool and then serve.

Nutrition (per Serving): Calories 157 Fat 13g Carbs 1.5g Protein 3.9g

Blueberry Lemon Custard Cake

Prep Time: 15 minutes | Cooking Time: 3 hours

Ingredients (3 Servings):

- 2 egg separated

- 2 tbsp fresh blueberries
- ½ cup light cream
- 1/8 tsp salt
- 2 tbsp Swerve sweetener
- ¼ tsp lemon liquid stevia
- 1 1/3 tbsp lemon juice
- ½ tsp lemon zest
- 2 tbsp coconut flour

Directions:

Put egg whites into a stand mixture and whip to achieve stiff peaks consistency. Set the egg whites aside, whisk the yolks and the other ingredients apart from the blueberries. Mix the egg whites into the batter to thoroughly combine, and then grease the slow cooker. Put the batter into it, then top with the blueberries. Cook within 3 hours, low. Let cool when not covered for 1 hour, then keep it chilled for at least 2 hours or overnight.

Serve the cake topped with unsweetened cream if you like.

Nutrition (per Serving): Calories 140 Fat 9.2g Carbs 2.3g Protein 8.9g

Slow-Cooked Pumpkin Custard

Prep Time: 15 minutes | Cooking Time: 3 hours

Ingredients (3 Servings):

- 2 large eggs
- 2 tbsp butter or coconut oil
- a dash of sea salt
- ½ tsp pumpkin pie spice
- ¼ cup superfine almond flour
- ½ tsp vanilla extract
- ½ cup pumpkin puree
- ¼ cup granulated stevia

Directions:

Grease a slow cooker with butter or coconut oil and set aside. With a mixer, break the eggs into a mixing bowl, and blend until incorporated and thickened.

Gently beat in the stevia, then add in vanilla extract and pumpkin puree. Then blend in pumpkin pie spice, salt, and almond flour. Once almost incorporated, stream in coconut oil, ghee, and melted butter. Mix until smooth, then move the mixture into a slow cooker.

Put a paper towel over the slow cooker to help absorb condensed moisture and prevent it from dripping on your pumpkin custard. Then cover with a lid.

Now cook on low for 2 hours to 2 hours 45 minutes and check the content after two hours elapse. Serve the custard with whipped cream sweetened with a little stevia and a sprinkle of nutmeg if you like.

Nutrition (per Serving): Calories 187 Fat 15g Carbs 5.4g Protein 6.5g

Almond Flour Fudge Cake

Prep Time: 15 minutes | Cooking Time: 4 hours

Ingredients (3 Servings):

- 1 egg
- 1/8 tsp Celtic Sea salt
- 1/3 tsp vanilla or chocolate extract
- 3 tbsp hot coffee
- 1/3 tsp baking soda
- 6 tbsp blanched almond flour
- 3 tbsp sour cream
- 3/4 oz unsweetened chocolate, melted
- 2 tbsp butter or coconut oil
- 6 tbsp Swerve

Directions:

Grease the slow cooker with oil. Then beat coconut oil and natural sweetener in a bowl until fully incorporated. Beat in eggs, cream and chocolate. In a bowl, sift baking soda and almond flour and add in the chocolate mixture. Then beat in coffee, salt, and vanilla until well incorporated. Once done, pour the batter into the cooking pot of the slow cooker.

Cook on low for 2 to 4 hours or until a toothpick inserted in the cake comes out clean.

Nutrition (per Serving): Calories 200 Carbs 5.8 Protein 6g Fat 18g

Slow cooker Bread Pudding

Prep Time: 15 minutes | Cooking Time: 5 hours

Ingredients (4 Servings):

- 1 egg white
- 1 whole egg
- 1 tbsp raisin
- ½ tsp cinnamon
- 1 ½ tsp vanilla extract
- 1/4 cup swerve
- 1 ½ cups almond milk
- 4 slices of pumpkin bread

Directions:

Slice the pumpkin bread into pieces. Then mix all the rest of the fixing in the slow cooker.

Cook within 4 to 5 hours, then serve.

Nutrition (per Serving): Calories 182 Fat 12g Carbs 5g Protein 4g

Tiramisu Bread Pudding

Prep Time: 15 minutes | Cooking Time: 2 hours

Ingredients (4 Servings):

- 1 large egg, beaten
- 3/4 tsp unsweetened cocoa
- 1/3 tsp vanilla extract
- 3 tbsp mascarpone cheese
- cooking spray
- 3 cups bread

- 6.4 oz almond milk, divided
- 3/4 tbsp Kahlua (coffee-flavored liqueur)
- 2 tsp instant espresso granules
- 3 tbsp coconut sugar
- 1.6 oz water

Directions:

Mix the water, coconut sugar, plus instant espresso granules in a saucepan. Boil while occasionally stirring for 1 minute, remove, then mix in the Kahlua liqueur. Whisk the eggs, then the almond milk in a large bowl. Mix in the espresso mixture into it. Put the Keto friendly bread into a greased casserole. Cook it inside the slow cooker within 2 hours, low. Mix vanilla, mascarpone cheese plus the remaining almond milk in a bowl. Garnish with cocoa and serve.

Nutrition (per Serving): Calories 139 Fat 9g Protein 6.7g Carbs 14g

Slow cooker Sugar-Free Dairy-Free Fudge

Prep Time: 15 minutes | Cooking Time: 2 hours

Ingredients (3 Servings):

- 1 tbsp coconut milk
- 4 tbsp sugar-free chocolate chips
- 1/4 tsp vanilla liquid stevia
- a dash of salt
- a dash of pure vanilla extract

Directions:

Mix in coconut milk, stevia, vanilla, chocolate chips plus salt in a slow cooker. Cook within 2 hours, then let it sit within 30 minutes. Mix in within 5 minutes. Put the batter in a casserole dish with parchment paper. Chill, then serve.

Nutrition (per Serving): Calories 45 Fat 5g Carbs 2g Protein 1g

Poppy Seed-Lemon Bread

Prep Time: 15 minutes | Cooking Time: 2 hours

Ingredients (3 Servings):

- 1 egg
- ¼ cup coconut sugar
- ½ cup almond flour
- ¼ tbsp baking powder
- 1 tbsp poppy seeds
- 1/8 tsp salt
- 2 tbsp vegetable oil
- 3 tbsp tofu (puree)
- ¼ cup almond milk
- 1 cup plain Greek-style yogurt
- ¼ cup lemon juice
- 3/4 tsp shredded lemon peel
- ¼ tsp vanilla

Directions:

Grease the slow cooker using a non-stick cooking spray. Mix the poppy seeds, flour, salt, and baking powder in a bowl, then put it aside. Mix the tofu puree, sugar, oil, milk, yogurt, lemon juice, lemon peel, and vanilla in a medium bowl. Put the sugar batter to the flour batter, then mix. Transfer it in the slow cooker, then cook on high for 1 and 30 minutes to 2 hours, or until set. Leave for 10-15 minutes to cool, then serve.

Nutrition (per Serving): Calories 195.6 Fat 14.3g Carbs 7.9g Protein 6.0g

Pumpkin Bread

Prep Time: 15 minutes | Cooking Time: 3 hours

Ingredients (4 Servings):

- 1 egg white
- 2 tbsp plain Greek yogurt
- ½ oz unsalted pecan pieces, toasted
- 1/4 tbsp pure vanilla extract
- 1 tbsp sunflower oil
- 1/4 cup cooked and puréed pumpkin
- 1/8 tsp sea salt
- a dash ground allspice
- 1/4 tsp ground nutmeg
- a dash tsp baking soda
- 1/2 tsp baking powder
- 2 tbsp coconut sugar
- 7 tbsp almond flour
- 2 tbsp dried apple cranberries, unsweetened
- 3 tbsp 100% apple juice, plain
- olive oil cooking spray

Directions:

Lightly grease a non-stick loaf pan with cooking spray. Set aside. Mix cranberries and apple juice in a small saucepan, heat the mixture on high to boil. Remove, then let cool for around 10 minutes. Then mix nutmeg, baking soda, allspice, baking powder, salt, maple sugar flakes, and flour in a large bowl. Set aside. Now mix vanilla, oil, egg whites, yogurt, pumpkin, and the cranberry mixture in a medium bowl. To the flour mixture, add the pecans and cranberry-pumpkin mixture and stir to incorporate fully. Spoon the batter into the pan and use a rubber spatula or back of a spoon to smooth the top. Arrange a rack inside a slow cooker to elevate the pan, and then put the pan on top. Cook within 3 hours, high. Cool it down within 10 minutes, before slicing, then serve.

Nutrition (per Serving): Calories 89 Carbs 3g Fat 6.5g Protein 4g

Baked Apples Recipe

Prep Time: 15 minutes | Cooking Time: 4 hours

Ingredients (6 Servings):

- 6 medium Gala apples
- ½ cup Quaker Old Fashioned Oats
- ½ cup Brown Sugar
- 3 tsp Cinnamon
- 2 tsp allspice
- 1/4 cup butter

Directions:

Pour 1/4 cup of water at slow cooker's edge. Use a sharp knife to carefully core apples.

Mix the oats, cinnamon, brown sugar, and allspice. Fill a single apple with a mixture of oats, sugar, and spice. Use a butter pat to top each apple. Set in slow cooker carefully and put the lid on slow cooker. Cook for 3–4 hours or until finished.

Nutrition (per Serving): Calories 208 Fat 8g Carbs 38g Protein 1g

Almond Butter and Chocolate Sauce

Prep Time: 15 minutes | Cooking Time: 4 hours

Ingredients (2 Servings):

- ½ cup almond butter
- 2 oz salted butter
- 1oz dark chocolate
- ½ tsp sea salt
- few drops of stevia

Directions:

Place the almond butter, butter, dark chocolate, sea salt, and stevia to the slow cooker. Cook for 4 hours, high, stirring every 30 minutes to combine the butter and chocolate as they melt. Serve or store in a fridge.

Nutrition (per Serving): Calories 562 Carbs 21g Fat 53g Protein 8.5g

Coconut Squares with Blueberry Glaze

Prep Time: 15 minutes | Cooking Time: 3 hours

Ingredients (8 Servings):

- 1 egg, beaten
- 2 cups dehydrated coconut
- 1 oz butter, melted
- 3 oz cream cheese
- ½ tsp baking powder
- 2 tsp vanilla extract
- 1 cup of frozen berries

Directions:

Beat the coconut, butter, cream cheese, egg, baking powder, and vanilla extract, using a wooden spoon in a bowl until combined and smooth. Grease a heat-proof dish with butter. Spread the coconut mixture into the dish. Defrost the blueberries in the microwave until they resemble a thick sauce. Spread the blueberries over the coconut mixture. Put the dish into the slow cooker, then put hot water until it reaches halfway up the dish. Cook for 3 hours, high. Remove the dish from the pot and leave to cool on the bench before slicing into small squares.

Nutrition (per Serving): Calories 115 Carbs 16g Fat 8g Protein 3g

Chocolate and Blackberry Cheesecake Sauce

Prep Time: 15 minutes | Cooking Time: 6 hours

Ingredients (2 Servings):

- ¾ lb. cream cheese
- ½ cup heavy cream
- 1 ½ oz butter

- 4 oz dark chocolate
- ½ cup fresh blackberries, chopped
- 1 tsp vanilla extract
- few drops of stevia

Directions:

Place the cream cheese, cream, butter, dark chocolate, blackberries, vanilla, and stevia into the slow cooker. Place the lid onto the pot and set the temperature to low. Cook for 6 hours, stirring every 30 minutes to combine the butter and chocolate as it melts. Serve, or store in a fridge.

Nutrition (per Serving): Calories 669 Carbs 38g Fat 53g Protein 13g

Berry & Coconut Cake

Prep Time: 15 minutes | Cooking Time: 2 hours

Ingredients (6 Servings):

- 1 large egg, beaten
- 1 tbsp butter for greasing the crock
- 1 cup almond flour
- ¾ cup sweetener of your choice
- 1 tsp baking soda
- ¼ tsp salt
- ¼ cup coconut flour
- ¼ cup coconut milk
- 3 tbsp coconut oil
- 4 cups fresh or frozen blueberries and raspberries

Directions:

Butter the slow cooker well. In a bowl, whisk the egg, coconut milk, and oil together. Mix the dry ingredients. Slowly stir in the wet ingredients. Do not over mix. Pour the batter in the slow cooker, spread evenly. Spread the berries on top. Cover, cook on high for 2 hours. Cool in the crock for 1-2 hours.

Nutrition (per Serving): Calories 183 Carbs 12g Fat 14g Protein 5g

Cocoa Pudding Cake

Prep Time: 15 minutes | Cooking Time: 3 hours

Ingredients (10 Servings):

- 3 large eggs
- 1 tbsp butter for greasing the slow cooker
- 1 ½ cups ground almonds
- ¾ cup sweetener, Swerve (or a suitable substitute)
- ¾ cup cocoa powder
- ¼ cup whey protein
- 2 tsp baking powder
- ¼ tsp salt
- ½ cup butter, melted
- ¾ cup full-fat cream
- 1 tsp vanilla extract

Directions:

Butter the slow cooker thoroughly. Whisk the dry fixing in a bowl. Stir in the melted butter, eggs, cream, and vanilla. Mix well. Pour the batter into the slow cooker and spread evenly. Cook within 2½ to 3 hours, low. If preferred – more like pudding, cook cake shorter; more dry cake, cook longer. Cool in the slow cooker for 30 minutes. Cut and serve.

Nutrition (per Serving): Calories 277 Carbs 11g Fat 25g Protein 7g

Wonderful Raspberry Almond Cake

Prep Time: 15 minutes | Cooking Time: 3 hours

Ingredients (4 Servings):

- 4 large eggs

- 1 cup fresh raspberries
- 1/3 cup   dark chocolate chips, sugar-free
- 2 cups almond flour
- 2 tsp coconut extract
- ¾ cup almond milk
- 2 tsp baking soda
- ¼ tsp salt
- 1 cup Swerve
- ½ cup melted coconut oil
- 1 cup shredded coconut unsweetened
- ¼ cup powdered egg whites

Directions:

Grease the slow cooker with butter. Mix all the fixing in a bowl. Pour the batter inslde, then cook within 3 hours on low. Serve.

Nutrition (per Serving): Calories 422 Carbs 17.8 g Fat 36g Protein 18g

Delicious Chocolate Cocoa Cake

Prep Time: 15 minutes | Cooking Time: 4 hours

Ingredients (4 Servings):

- 2 large eggs
- 1 ½ cups ground almonds
- ½ cup coconut flakes
- 5 tbsp your preferred sweetener

Nutrition (per Serving): Carbs 9 g Protein 17 g Fat 28g Calories 341

- 2 tsp baking powder
- a pinch salt
- ½ cup coconut oil
- ½ cup cooking cream
- 2 tbsp lemon juice
- the zest from 2 lemons
- Espresso and whipped cream for serving

Toppings:

- 3 tbsp of sweetener
- ½ a cup of boiling water
- 2 tbsp of lemon juice
- 2 tbsp of coconut oil

Directions:

Combine the baking powder, sweetener, coconut, and almonds in a large bowl. Whisk together thoroughly.   In another bowl, combine the eggs, juice, coconut oil, and whisk together thoroughly. Combine the wet and the dry ingredients and whisk together thoroughly.   Put the aluminum foil inside the bottom of the slow cooker. Pour the batter into the slow cooker. Mix all the topping fixing in a small bowl and pour on top of the cake batter.

Cover the slow cooker with paper towels to absorb condensation, then cook within 3 hours on high.   Divide into bowls and serve with espresso and whipped cream.

RECIPES INDEX

COOKING CHART

VOLUME EQUIVALENTS (LIQUID)

US STANDARD	US STD (OUNCES)	METRIC (approx)
2 tablespoons	1 fl.oz.	30 ml
¼ cup	2 fl.oz.	60 ml
½ cup	4 fl.oz.	120 ml
1 cup	8 fl.oz.	240 ml
1 ½ cup	12 fl.oz.	355 ml
2 cup or 1 pint	16 fl.oz.	475 ml
4 cup or 1 quart	32 fl.oz.	1 L
1 gallon	128 fl.oz.	4 L

OVEN TEMPERATURES

FAHRENHEIT (F)	CELSIUS (approx)
250° F	120° C
300° F	150° C
325° F	165° C
350° F	180° C
375° F	190° C
400° F	200° C
425° F	220° C
450° F	230° C

VOLUME EQUIVALENTS (DRY)

US STANDARD	METRIC (approx)
¼ teaspoon	1 ml
½ teaspoon	2 ml
¾ teaspoon	4 ml
1 teaspoon	5 ml
1 tablespoon	15 ml
¼ cup	60 ml
1/3 cup	80 ml
½ cup	120 ml
1 cup	240 ml
2 cup or 1 pint	475 ml
3 cup	700 ml
4 cup or 1 quart	1 L

WEIGHT EQUIVALENTS

US STANDARD	METRIC (approx)
½ ounce	15 g
1 ounce	30 g
2 ounces	60 g
4 ounces	115 g
8 ounces	225 g
12 ounces	340 g
16 ounces or 1 pound	455 g

Made in the USA
Las Vegas, NV
23 November 2022

59952966R00074